TE DUE

THE ETERNAL SOLITARY

Eternal solitaries—human souls,
Solitaries blown astray;
Each wanders through the Milky Way,
Each in its finite circle rolls.

ANTONI LANGE[1]

The Eternal Solitary

A STUDY OF JOSEPH CONRAD

by

ADAM GILLON

BOOKMAN ASSOCIATES, INC. • NEW YORK

Library of Congress Catalog Card Number: 60–14919

2nd printing..................... *1966*

MANUFACTURED IN THE UNITED STATES OF AMERICA

For

GONYA *and* ISABELLA

PREFACE

The following pages are a study of isolation as a dominant *motif* in the life and works of Joseph Conrad. As a serious novelist, Conrad was not interested in *categories* of isolation such as a literary critic may devise for the convenience of his argument; yet even a cursory acquaintance with his work immediately shows his fascination with "isolatoes." In order to impose a certain pattern of classification upon them it would be desirable to adopt some broad definition of the term involved. It was coined by Melville in describing the crew of the Pequod: "They were nearly all Islanders . . . 'Isolatoes' too . . . not acknowledging the common continent of men, but each isolato living on a separate continent of his own."[2] An isolato in Conrad's works is a man incapable of living the kind of life he wishes to live, through adverse circumstances or through his own faults. If he is a man of achievement, he cannot bring it to consummation; if he has failed in his projects, he cannot forget his weakness; if he has committed an act of treachery, he is tortured by a morbid sense of remorse, and lives only to redeem his crime, or what *he* considers to be a crime. Often he is overwhelmed by the contrast of what he is and what he dreams of being. Thrown upon himself, the isolated man forever faces an impassable wall that separates him even from the people who stand closest to him.

Joseph Conrad was such an isolated man himself. He knew the anguish of exile and the despair of a household beset by a spectre of implacable tragedy. He learned the meaning of moral isolation after he left Poland against the wishes of his relatives, leaving behind his first love, a girl who was a model of patriotism. The young sailor found adventure on the high seas and in the mysterious jungles of the East, but when the spell of romance was gone, it was followed by gloomy disenchantment and crushing solitude. For Conrad could not share his dreams with the other members of the crew, nor with anybody else. He discovered the loneliness of command and the heart of darkness in the wilderness of the Congo. Finally, for almost thirty years he knew the alienation of the creative artist.

He drew heavily on his own experiences, even directly transcribing into his books events and the names of the people whom he met during his voyages. And since his experiences as sailor and writer only enhanced the condition of loneliness, to which Conrad was predisposed by his background and temperament, it is small wonder that his work shows a veritable procession of isolatoes.

NOTE: *For technical reasons, "diacritical signs," representing distinctive pronunciation of certain Polish sounds, are omitted.*

ACKNOWLEDGMENTS

I wish to thank Professors Marjorie Nicolson, Susanne H. Nobbe and William York Tindall, of the Graduate Department of English, Columbia University, for their encouragement and critical suggestions.

I am indebted to Professor Ludwik Krzyzanowski, editor of *The Polish Review,* for permission to quote from his articles, "Joseph Conrad's 'Prince Roman'" and "Joseph Conrad: Some Polish Documents."

I am grateful to Dr. Watson Kirkconnell, President of Acadia University, for a grant which paid part of the typing costs.

Dr. Herbert Lewis of Acadia University deserves my thanks for his valuable ideas and help with the proofreading of the manuscript.

Short portions of this book have appeared in *The Polish Review* and *The Dalhousie Review,* and are printed with the kind permisssion of the editors.

Thanks are due to the following publishing houses for permission to quote from the works listed:

J. M. Dent & Sons, Ltd. (London): *Joseph Conrad, Edition of the Complete Works,* Jean-Aubry, *Joseph Conrad: Life and Letters, The Sea Dreamer* (all published in the U.S. by Doubleday & Co.).

McGraw-Hill Book Co., Inc. (New York): Jocelyn Baines, *Joseph Conrad: A Critical Biography.*

Methuen & Co. Ltd. (London): Jean-Paul Sartre, *Existentialism and Humanism.*

G. P. Putnam's Sons (New York): Jerry Allen, *The Thunder and the Sunshine*.

New Directions (New York): Jean-Paul Sartre, *Nausea, Intimacy* (reprinted in an Avon edition by permission of New Directions; all rights reserved).

CONTENTS

THE ETERNAL SOLITARY

CHAPTER I

THE INCORRIGIBLE
DON QUIXOTE

I . . . have been called an incorrigible Don Quixote.[1]

Our enemies . . . have bestowed upon us the epithet of "Incorrigible."[2]

CONRAD'S EARLY YEARS were marked by sadness and loneliness. He grew up in the atmosphere of national defeat and frustration that followed the ill-omened Polish insurrection of 1863. Tsarist Russia ruled Poland with an iron hand, suppressing every display of nationalism, even forbidding the teaching of Polish language. Savage retribution met any attempt at national self-expression and organization.

Both Conrad's parents came from families that sacrificed property, liberty and life on behalf of the Polish struggle for independence. His father, Apollo Korzeniowski, was exiled to Vologda, in Northern Russia, for alleged participation in a secret national committee. He was accompanied there by his wife and son, who had to accept the discipline

15

administered to the prisoner. The journey and exile broke
the frail health of Evelina, Conrad's mother, and she died
of consumption in 1865. His father succumbed four years
later, leaving the boy in the care of Tadeusz Bobrowski,
Evelina's brother. Conrad was an orphan at the age of
twelve.

Toward the end of his life Apollo Korzeniowski became
a gloomy man, driven by despair into religious fanaticism.
The years spent at the side of this sad dying man, without
friends of his own age, without moments of childish gaiety,
must have left a deep imprint on Conrad's mind. There was
one scene in particular, which made an indelible impression
on his youthful memory—the sight of Apollo Korzeniowski
supervising the burning of his papers shortly before he died;
so indelible that he recalled it with minute detail forty-six
years later. He was profoundly affected by this act of surrender. His father was a vanquished man.

This memory may have something to do with Conrad's
habit of tearing and burning his manuscripts. One wonders
whether it also inspired him when he described the burning
of Almayer's house. Almayer, it will be recalled, wanted to
destroy this symbol of his love for his daughter who had
betrayed him. If Conrad did think of his father, he certainly
disguised Almayer's intentions. Almayer destroys the last
vestige of Nina's existence solely out of weakness and a
desire to attain oblivion. Apollo Korzeniowski also wanted
to forget, but in spite of his being mortally weary he was
not afraid of death. Death was no enemy to a man of such
strong faith. Almayer, on the other hand, feared the approaching end.

When we look for characters whom Conrad may have
drawn after the image of his father, or at least whom he
has patterned on "the ardent fidelity of the man whose life
had been a fearless confession in word and deed of a creed
which the simplest heart . . . could feel and understand," [3]
we must think more of the old faithful sailors of Conrad

(and men like Lord Jim) than of Almayer. But the feeling stirred in the young man as a result of his father's martyrdom was permanently graven in his heart. It was

. . . that appalling feeling of inexorable fate, tangible, palpable, a figure of dread, murmuring with iron lips the final words: Ruin—and Extinction.[4]

These words were written in 1915, when Conrad was a mature artist. Twenty years earlier, he said the same thing in his first Author's Note to *Almayer's Folly*. The mood of resignation pervades this book and many other novels and stories. It is a true, basic emotion for Conrad.

Resignation, not mystic, not detached, but resignation open-eyed, conscious, and informed by love, is the only one of our feelings for which it is impossible to become a sham.[5]

Apollo Korzeniowski feared that the harsh realities of the exile might impair his son's emotional life and freeze his young heart. But Conrad's heart was not withered. Fortunately, he was a reading boy, and a creative reader at that. Endowed with a rich imagination and an unusual sensitivity, young Conrad reacted to the oppressive atmosphere of his household and to the conditions of exile as his heroes did to their privations—he withdrew into himself. He was a solitary, nostalgic child, greatly resembling his father in his moods of total immersion in his own imaginative life.

I don't know what would have become of me if I had not been a reading boy. . . . I suppose that in a futile, childish way I would have gone crazy. But I was a reading boy. . . . I read! What did I not read! [6]

There is no doubt that Conrad's early reading fare was greatly responsible for his dream of the sea. He admired Marryat's *Masterman Ready* and *Midshipman Easy*, Fenimore Cooper's *The Last of the Mohicans*. He was fascinated by Captain R. N. McClintock's *The Voyage of the "Fox" in the Arctic Seas* (a Narrative of the Discovery of the Fate of Sir John Franklin and His Companions) and, while his father lay desperately ill, he read about three Scottish explorers in Africa, James Bruce, Mungo Park and David Livingstone. Of the French authors, Louis Ambroise Garneray, artist and sailor, was his favorite; Conrad read his *Récits, Aventures et Combats.* When he was only eight years old he read to his father the proofs of his translation of Victor Hugo's *Travailleurs de la Mer* (Toilers of the Sea) and Alfred de Vigny's *Chatterton.* He also perused his father's translations of Shakespeare's *The Two Gentlemen of Verona, Much Ado About Nothing, As You Like It, A Comedy of Errors* and *Othello.* (One recalls that Lord Jim carries a tattered edition of the Bard on his journeys.) He read Walter Scott, Byron, Thackeray and Trollope. He was a great admirer of Dickens, singling out *Bleak House* as

. . . a work of the master for which I have such an admiration, or rather such an intense and unreasoning affection, dating from the days of my childhood, that its very weaknesses are more precious to me than the strength of other men's work. I have read it innumerable times, *both in Polish and in English;* I have read it only the other day . . .[7]

He devoured history, voyages and novels of adventure in Polish and French. He knew *Gil Blas* and was particularly fond of *Don Quixote,* a fact noted by his collaborator Ford Madox Ford (Hueffer) who also adds that Conrad was very partial to his own sea Don Quixote, Lingard.

Failing to dissuade Conrad from his wish to go to sea, his tutor, Adam Pulmann, called him "an incorrigible, hopeless Don Quixote." Conrad recalled the incident many years later:

I was surprised. I was only fifteen and did not know what he meant exactly. But I felt vaguely flattered at the name of the immortal knight turning up in connection with my own folly, as some people would call it to my face.[8]

The boy's quixotic dreams precipitated a conflict with his community and, what was even more momentous for the shaping of his character, a conflict with himself. Conrad's relatives voiced their indignation at his seafaring plans, and probably he himself saw that his pursuit of a sailor's career could not be reconciled with his birth and the tradition of Polish landowners. Neither could it be reconciled with the ideals of Polish patriotism. He had been very close to his father whose main ambition in his last years of life was making Joseph a good Pole. The inscription on Apollo Korzeniowski's gravestone read:

TO APOLLO KORZENIOWSKI
VICTIM OF MUSCOVITE TYRANNY
Born Feb. 23, 1820
Died May 23, 1869
TO THE MAN WHO LOVED HIS COUNTRY
WORKED FOR IT AND DIED FOR IT
HIS COMPATRIOTS

Conrad's family was not anxious to have him remain a Russian subject, always suspected by the authorities, but the boy could have lived in the part of Poland occupied by Austria. After his father's death in Cracow (where Conrad went to school), the freedom of the city was conferred upon him, thus making him eligible for Austrian nationality. In fact, in later years, Tadeusz Bobrowski, Conrad's maternal uncle, urged him to become an Austrian subject. The adventurous youth, however, could not follow his dreams in the city of Cracow; like the knight of La Mancha he could not be a good citizen of his country. He recognized this clearly, but he was hurt by charges of treason and desertion.

I have the conviction that there are men of unstained rectitude who are ready to murmur scornfully the word desertion. Thus the taste of innocent adventure may be made bitter to the palate. The part of the inexplicable should be allowed in appraising the conduct of men in a world where no explanation is final. No charge of faithlessness ought to be lightly uttered. . . . The fidelity to a special tradition may last through the events of an unrelated existence, following faithfully, too, the traced way of an inexplicable impulse.[9]

To a sensitive boy between fifteen and sixteen the commotion stirred in his little world by his decision had seemed a very big thing indeed. Thirty-five years later he still pondered on it. The magnitude of that commotion may be partly responsible for Conrad's attitude toward seamanship. He left Poland, proving to himself and to his uncle that he could master his profession; similarly, after he abandoned his career as a sailor he again had to justify his existence by being successful in his second great adventure, when once more he obeyed the mysterious impulse—to become an English writer. While this conflict does account, in some measure, for so many of Conrad's isolatoes who seek moral redemption, it would be over-simplification to identify his emigration from Poland with *all* acts of treason committed by his protagonists. The things that matter to us at this point are Conrad's determination to be successful in his career and his subsequent disillusionment as he struggled for recognition as sailor and artist.

The long interlude of the sea years brought him great moments of wonder and excitement. Since the romantic feeling of reality was in him an inborn faculty (as he admitted himself) the young sailor did not have to wait long to find the romance of youth, the fascination of remote lands and the spirit of adventure. The sea life made a man of the impressionable, romantic youth and molded his character and convictions. Despite the obstacles in his way— the language barrier, his background, and his health, he learned how to be a resolute and efficient sea-captain. What then were the circumstances during his sea years that turned the exaltation and enthusiasm of the young sailor into the frustration and bitterness which we find in him at the outset of his writing career?

To answer this question let us briefly examine the following elements in his sea life: the nature of Conrad's passion for the sea; the frustration of a lost romantic cause; the hardships of the vocation and how they affected Conrad; his poverty and the struggle for a berth; the unromantic aspects of some exploits; disease and suffering as a result of his travels; the loneliness and isolation of the deck.

Conrad cut a strange figure among the tough sea-wolves of his day. He dressed and bore himself like a Polish nobleman, and the crew of the *Saint-Antoine,* on which he sailed in 1877, dubbed him "The Count" (and also "The Russian Count"). But it was not merely his external appearance that made him so different. There may have been some romantic sailors among the men of his calling, but it is highly doubtful whether there was one soul among the Lingards, the MacWhirrs, the Whalleys and the Anthonys of the real life, who regarded the seaman's vocation as a passion "various and great like life itself." [10] Even the adventurous Dominic Cervoni of Conrad's Marseilles days, who, according to Conrad, was his true initiator into the life of the sea, had few illusions about his profession and usually curbed the impetuous plans of his eager pupil. Neither Dominic nor any sailor of Conrad's acquaintance could possibly have shared his vehement passion for the sea, and none was made as lonely as Conrad was by the intensity of his emotions. In *The Mirror of the Sea,* one of his most autobiographical books, he analyzes the nature of his infatuation:

. . . if anybody suggests that this must be the lyric illusion of an old, romantic heart, I can answer that for twenty years I had lived *like a hermit with my passion!* Beyond the line of the sea horizon the *world for me did not exist* as assuredly as it does not exist for the mystics who take refuge on the top of high mountains. I am speaking now of that innermost life, containing

the best and the worst that can happen to us in the tempera-
mental depths of our being, *where a man indeed must live
alone* . . .[11]

Like Lord Jim, Conrad found the life at sea enticing,
but in all his speculation about adventure the reward that
is found in the perfect love of one's duty eluded him. His
dreams of valorous deeds seemed to be the essence of his
life and its hidden reality. Such romanticism carries within
its shell the bitter fruit of disappointment.

Conrad shared with Don Quixote the inexplicable impulse that drives a man to self-indulgence. The Spanish
hidalgo wished to encounter the noble giant Brandabarban,
and Conrad, the boy, put his finger on the blank space on
the map, which to him represented the unsolved mystery of
Africa, and said to himself that he would go there when he
grew up. He did. But his long voyages led him into the
Heart of Darkness, where the ardor of youth was trans-
formed into a very different feeling. When Conrad left the
sea, he still cherished a filial regard for the simple men
who had for ages traversed it. He had, however, experienced a revelation that shattered the illusion of tragic
dignity which men's self-respect had cast over their tussle
with the sea:

On that exquisite day . . . *perished my romantic love* to what
men's imagination had proclaimed the most august aspect of
Nature. *The cynical indifference of the sea* to the merits of
human suffering and courage, laid bare in this ridiculous, panic-
tainted performance extorted from the dire extremity of nine
good and honorable seamen, revolted me. I saw the duplicity of
the sea's most tender mood. It was so because it could not help
itself, but *the awed respect* of *the early days was gone*. I felt
ready *to smile bitterly* at its enchanting charm and glare vici-
ously at its furies. In a moment . . . I had *looked coolly* at the
life of my choice. *Its illusions were gone*, but its fascination
remained.[12]

Actually, the first blow to Conrad's illusions was dealt not by the sea but by his unfortunate participation, without political interest or passion, in the hopeless cause of Carlism. The Poles have a long tradition of fighting for lost causes, particularly in the days of their great romantic literature. Polish literature abounds in heroes sacrificing their lives chivalrously for a cause doomed to failure. A few years before his death Conrad commented on the nature of the Carlist enterprise in a letter to a critic, calling it "a very straightforward adventure conducted with inconceivable stupidity and *a foredoomed failure* from the first." [13] But at the time Conrad joined a gun-running band, serving the interests of the Carlist dynasty, the undertaking seemed the ideal answer to Conrad's quest for excitement and romantic adventure. It was a dangerous business, and its chief virtue lay in the deliberate risk which the gun-runners were taking; otherwise, it was a very dull affair which culminated in disaster and a profound shock to the young man. The mood of those days is captured in *The Arrow of Gold*, a book almost as autobiographical as *The Mirror of the Sea*. *The Arrow* provides a good illustration of the sad experience Conrad had to undergo time and again—the discovery of the great chasm between dream and reality.

The little vessel, broken and gone like the only toy of a lonely child, the sea itself, which had swallowed it, throwing me on shore after a shipwreck that *instead of a fair fight left in me the memory of a suicide*. It took away all that there was in me of independent life. Even Dominic failed me, *his moral entity destroyed.* . . . I found myself weary, heartsore, my brain still dazed and with awe in my heart entering Marseilles by way of the railway station, *after many adventures, one more disagreeable than another,* involving *privations, great exertions, a lot of difficulties* with all sorts of people who looked upon me evidently more as *a discreditable vagabond* deserving the attentions of gendarmes than a respectable *(if crazy)* young gentleman attended by a guardian angel of his own. I must confess that I slunk out of the railway station shunning its many lights as if, invariably, *failure made an outcast of a man*.[14]

Suicide, loneliness, disagreeable adventures, privations, great exertions, discreditable vagabond, and outcast—these were hardly the attributes of a great romantic adventure. And his love affair with the mysterious Doña "Rita," which followed the gun-running episode, may have given him some ecstatic moments of happiness, but it ended abruptly and painfully.

The affair with "Rita," so vividly recalled by Conrad at the age of sixty in *The Arrow of Gold,* still presents a knotty issue for the biographers of Conrad. Jean-Aubry regards *The Arrow of Gold* as fully autobiographical, professing ignorance as to the real name of Rita de Lastaola. We thus have the figure of Monsieur George as the young Conrad who returns after the loss of the *Tremolino* and is finally accepted by "Rita." They retire to a secluded village in the Maritime Alps for an idyllic and totally isolated existence. The period of their intense happiness is brief, probably the last two weeks of 1877 and the beginning months of 1878. Conrad leaves the village for a short trip to Marseilles to draw his income. While he is there a Royalist friend tells him that Captain J. M. K. Blunt (who described himself as *Américain, catholique et gentilhomme*) has been spreading rumors about Madame de Lastaola having fallen "into the hands of an unscrupulous young adventurer whom she was keeping." [15] Whereupon Conrad challenges Blunt, and the two meet in a duel late in February, 1878. Conrad wounds Blunt in the right hand. Blunt fires with his left, wounding Conrad in the left side of his breast bone. Notified by Conrad's German friend, Richard Fecht, Tadeusz Bobrowski travels to Marseilles. Meanwhile, Conrad is being nursed by "Rita," who leaves him when he is out of danger. Uncle Tadeusz arrives in Marseilles, pays the young man's debts, scolds him for his folly and goes back to the Ukraine with a stern warning to Conrad to stay within his income of twenty-four hundred francs a year.

In his recent biography, Mr. Jocelyn Baines deals with the discrepancies of this account.[16] Mr. Baines contends that Conrad's duel never took place, but that Conrad attempted suicide, shooting himself after having gambled away his money in Monte Carlo. This thesis is based on a long-lost letter from Tadeusz Bobrowski to a friend of Conrad's father, Stefan Buszczynski. The letter relates how Conrad tried to kill himself with a revolver and how Bobrowski has told everyone that his nephew was wounded in a duel. The letter was discovered by a Polish critic, Zdzislaw Najder (who has written articles on Conrad and is working on a biography of Conrad) to whom Mr. Baines imparted his doubts about Conrad's duel.

Why did Conrad try to kill himself? Was it only because of his loss of the money lent to him by Fecht? Or was it the unhappy conclusion of his love affair with "Rita" or both? Was he trying to regain "Rita" by way of a "rigged" suicide (as Mr. Baines suggests)? No final answer can be given to these questions; moreover, Bobrowski's letter and the two other references to the shooting in Marseilles[17] are not eyewitness accounts but merely what Bobrowski learned from Conrad himself and from his friends. It should also be noted that although Conrad's son John confirms the fact of his father's having had a scar in the left breast (an indication that, being right-handed, he could hardly have been hit in the left side), both he and his brother Borys refused to accept Baines's version of the incident.

Mr. Baines declares that certain people disagree with him,[18] but he does not give any account of the controversy. He mentions Miss Jerry Allen's biography of Conrad in connection with the identification of "Rita," but omits to discuss her counter-argument on the subject of Conrad's attempted suicide.

Miss Allen has no doubts about Conrad's duel with Blunt. She quotes from a Polish document called "For the information of my dear nephew Konrad Korzeniowski," a notebook of 22 pages, handwritten by Tadeusz Bobrowski, which indicates clearly that Conrad's wound was not the result of an attempted suicide but obviously the outcome of his duel. He makes the following entry:

In February, 1878, in Kiev I received from M. Bonnard a demand to pay your promissory note for 1,000 francs and almost simultaneously news from M. Fecht *that you were in a shooting* . . .[19]

As the purpose of this notebook was to preserve for Conrad information about his parents and to provide a record of his expenses and activities during the period December 1, 1869 and February 4, 1890, it is very difficult to find a logical explanation why it should contain a lie.

Miss Allen also cites the letter to Stefan Buszczynski, but gives it an interpretation that is totally different from that of Mr. Baines.

Called upon to explain his nephew's close-to-the-heart wound a year later in the Ukraine, Thaddeus Bobrowski wrote an account of it, "the germ of Conrad's story," on March 24, 1879 to Stefan Buszczynski, an old friend of the family. His letter revealed the confused myth Conrad had woven to camouflage his romance. According to his uncle's report, Conrad had been unable to undertake his world voyage with Captain Escarras because of French passport regulations; failing in that, he had been talked into a smuggling affair by Captain Duteil of the *Mont-Blanc* [who being off on a voyage could not be questioned]; losing financially in the smuggling escapade, Conrad had attempted, unsuccessfully, to join the American navy at Villefrance; disappointed there and without funds, he had borrowed 800 francs from Richard Fecht but gambled it away at Monte Carlo; in despair over his money problems, he had attempted suicide, shooting himself with a revolver. . . . "I never could invent an effective lie," Conrad was to write to his friend, R. B. Cunninghame Graham, twenty years later. Yet the yarn he told his uncle, allied as it was with finances—the core of his uncle's interests—was convincing enough for Thaddeus Bobrowski to relate it. That he, even then, disbelieved Conrad's tale of suicide attempt came out in his notebook entry—written for Conrad, alone, to read—where he referred to his nephew's being "in a shooting," his sarcastic term for "the duel, he concluded the same perplexed letter to Buszczynski in which he recounted the overly romantic myth of Conrad's tea-hour, self-inflicted wound. He knew only too well how lightly his nephew took financial problems, the debts he had never been without during three and a half years of carefree living. But, lacking any hint of the true reason for the duel, the practical accountant-minded Thaddeus could only ascribe money losses as the motive for the youth—a sympathetic "character" who was "ardent and original" in his imagination and talk, as he described Conrad to Buszczynski—guarding a private hurt, far beyond the older man's understanding.[20]

If Miss Allen's emphasis on the phrase "you were in a shooting," refers to the Polish *zes sie postrzelil* (that you shot yourself) then, obviously, she is wrong and Mr. Baines has the correct translation. The latter doubts that Conrad lied about his attempted suicide, for there was nothing disreputable about duels in those days, particularly for a descendant of Polish landed gentry. Baines charges the "clingers to the duel version" with an attempt to advance the improbable proposition that Conrad lied to Bobrowski, who then invented the truth. Perhaps the idea seems improbable, but it is *possible*. For example, Conrad might have wanted to soften his uncle's heart with the story of his suicide.

Mr. Baines correctly stresses the psychological importance of an attempted suicide:

An attempt to kill oneself would in all circumstances be a traumatic experience; and this would have been particularly intense in Conrad's case because, according to the Roman Catholic dogma under which he had been brought up, attempted suicide is a mortal sin.[21]

However, this is a bit of a simplification in Conrad's case, for, in Mr. Baines's own words,

Although he was born and brought up a Roman Catholic, and his father was an almost mystical believer, he rejected Christianity. . . . He said: "It's strange how I always, from the age of fourteen, disliked the Christian religion, its doctrines, ceremonies and festivals."[22]

Whatever the cause of the wound which Conrad sustained in Marseilles, it is quite possible that Conrad was driven to attempt suicide (or to a duel) by his affair with "Rita," whom Miss Allen identifies as Paula de Somoggy (or Somogyi). She was not a Basque, as Conrad described her in *The Mirror of the Sea*, but a Hungarian peasant girl who was raised in her native hills by her uncle, a parish priest. When she was eighteen she was "discovered" by Don Carlos who fell in love with her and took her to Paris. There she was presented as the favorite of "the King" under the assumed name of Baroness Paula de Somoggy. Miss Allen cites from the memoirs of the Count de Melgar,[23] a Spanish aristocrat who served as secretary to Don Carlos for twenty years, whose description of Paula is very close to Conrad's portrait of Rita. Paula de Somoggy, it appears, was not only a strikingly beautiful blond woman; she was also endowed with an extraordinary intelligence. She learned to speak five European languages and carried herself with royal grace. Her career "became a true story in the vein of *Pygmalion* which George Bernard Shaw was to write thirty-five years later."[24]

Mr. Baines discards this identification, pointing out that it has been made on very flimsy evidence. His picture of Paula is quite different and, on the basis of chronology alone, it is

. . . virtually impossible that Paula was the "Rita" in Conrad's life. She arrived on the scene much too late for this and was, moreover, very much under Don Carlo's wing. It is most improbable that Conrad had the opportunity of meeting her, let alone of having an affair with her. There is no evidence of her going to Marseilles, and why should she have gone there? Don Carlos had clearly lost interest in his own cause and, besides, even he would scarcely have used as his emissary a young Hungarian chorus-girl, who knew, apart from her own language, only a little German.[25]

It is clear that the two views of Paula clash. While some of Mr. Baines's objections to Miss Allen's portrait of Paula are justified, he has not disproved her contention that Paula de Somoggy was very talented and knew several languages; and, of course, his case would be perfect if he could produce the identity of the real "Rita." As it is, even Mr. Baines reluctantly admits certain similarities between the life of Paula and that of "Rita."

Whoever "Rita" was, the love affair with her was a most important event in Conrad's life; he could never forget her. And, perhaps, like the young George of *The Arrow of Gold,* he looked at all women "and each reminded him of Doña Rita, either by some profound resemblance or by the startling force of contrast."[26] "Rita" was not the first love of young Conrad. Several years earlier (in September of 1873) he had suffered the pangs of an unrequited teen-age love for a Polish girl who must have humiliated him severely. The incident is described in a deleted passage from *The Arrow of Gold,* and its echoes can be heard in many an anguished cry of Conrad's unlucky lovers.

From the nature of things first love can never be a wholly happy experience. But this man seems to have been exceptionally unlucky. His conviction is that, in colloquial phrase, he had struck something particularly wicked and even devilish. He holds that belief after thirty-five years, and positively shudders at the mere recollection. . . . Stupid people are very prone to turn a genuine display of sentiment into ridicule—and, women, of course, have special opportunities in this way. . . . She amused herself again by tormenting him privately and publicly with great zest and method and finally 'executed' him in circumstances of peculiar atrocity—which don't matter here. . . .

He came out of it *seamed, scarred, almost flayed* and with a *complete distrust of himself,* an abiding fear. . . .[27]

Conrad's second love was his eighteen-year-old cousin, Tekla Syroczynska. Although this affair did not result in humiliation for him, it was not a happy experience either. Jocelyn Baines asserts that Conrad's allusions to his childhood love-life are contradictory. His first romantic heroworship was a girl called Janina Taube. It is she, rather than Tekla Syroczynska, who served as a model for Antonia of *Nostromo.* As failure in adolescent loves could have been partly responsible for his desire to leave his native country, so the end of the affair with "Rita" certainly made him wish to escape the atmosphere of Marseilles. He was resolved to leave the city, now embarking on a career of a sailor rather than indulging in mere adventure. The man who boarded the Scottish ship *Mavis* in 1878 to voyage to Lowestoft was no longer the starry-eyed youth seeking the thrills of romantic exploits. He was nineteen years old, however; and at this age it is not difficult to feel exhilarated even if one is very lonely. After a period of probation and training as ordinary seaman on board a North Sea coaster, Conrad arrived from Lowestoft to London.

. . . with something of the feeling of a traveller penetrating into a vast and unexplored wilderness. *No explorer could have been more lonely.* I did not know a single soul of all these millions that all around me peopled the mysterious distances of the streets. . . . *I was elated.* I was pursuing a clear aim, I was carrying out a deliberate plan of making out of myself, in the first place a *seaman worthy of the service,* good enough to work by the side of the men with whom I was to live; and in the second place, *I had to justify my existence to myself, to redeem*

a tacit moral pledge. Both these aims were to be attained by
the same effort. How simple seemed the problem of life then,
on that hazy day of early September in the year 1878, when
I entered London for the first time.

From that point of view—*Youth* and a straightforward
scheme of conduct—it was certainly a year of grace.[28]

In these lines Conrad offers a good example of the con-
flicting elements in his nature: the youthful, romantic feeling of reality (which he captured so beautifully in "Youth")
and feeling for moral values in man's life, even when the
latter appears empty or futile. Thus, still in the grip of his
adolescent passion for the sea and with the realization of
a moral obligation to himself and his profession, he set
about the goal of becoming an officer of the merchant
marine. It was no easy task for a man of his temperament,
and it required the singular tenacity of will and purpose
which he maintained throughout his life. The struggle of
the crew against the treachery of the sea filled him with
exaltation, but the prosaic severity of the daily routine
aboard ship were too trivial and dull for the young Pole.
He had expected to find a new adventure in each voyage;
instead, the long months spent in the isolation of the sea,
often in the company of men with whom he had nothing
in common, revived the slumbering nostalgia which was
ever present in him. The fatigue of work, coupled with his
linguistic difficulties, also contributed to a certain feeling
of weariness and melancholy that was to stay with him for
the rest of his life.

Conrad's preoccupation with failure in his books is not
surprising since he knew the meaning of the word quite
well. His letters bear ample evidence of plans that failed,
of his exasperation at being often without a berth. His
financial ventures did not succeed. The voyages brought
him scanty remuneration and no prospect of security. Not
that he longed for wealth and extravagance. But poverty,
boredom, dreariness—were these to be his lot on this earth?

Was this existence the realization of his great dream? He replied in the negative to these tormenting questions, scarcely knowing that the worst had yet to come. For it was in the mysterious Congo that he really suffered the most severe shock. Instead of romance he found the horror of the jungle and its savage laws, the utter degradation of man isolated in the wilderness. The scramble for loot, the immorality of Belgian explorers and traders filled him with disgust. He had no point of contact with all these men.

During his early escapades, like the truly romantic voyage to the Gulf of Mexico, Conrad rarely stopped to analyze his fellow sailors. Their very faults had been a source of gratification. But the mature seaman saw the frailties of human nature and pondered on them with feelings of bitterness, gloom and resignation. He began to question the existence of any purpose in life, which he found full of unextinguishable regrets. The adventure in the Congo, which had once inflamed his childish imagination, he found to be gray, somber, struggle for survival, a most unexciting contest which offered neither glory nor victory.

The Congo voyage also had another effect on Conrad: it seriously impaired his health. Frequent spells of ill-health enhanced his habit of reverie and often made him feel demoralized. It is small wonder that with perfect sincerity he sometimes wished himself dead. He yielded to haunting memories and vague regrets. He reflected on his disappointed hopes and the rather poor consolation that one must live when one has had the misfortune to be born. He began to be aware of a certain duality in himself, another "I" who could be in two places at once. The romantic sailor had turned into a lonely thinker with a passion for introspection. His concern was now with his own fate and that of humanity, with the meaning of failure and success, fidelity and faithfulness. Conrad the sailor was dead, and out of his misery and disenchantment Conrad the writer was born.

The transition did not take place suddenly. It evolved out of a serious inner crisis that Conrad experienced toward the end of his sea years, something he called "the shadow line." It was a time when his impulses seemed to him as inscrutable as the cruelty of man's destiny. His dreams turned into nightmares, his life into a kind of vegetation. Baffled by his own nature he went back to his past for clues, but he found no solution to his doubts save for the realization that the individual in the scheme of the universe was utterly insignificant and life in general was abominably sad. Yet for all his irascibility and unhappiness Conrad never succumbed to the stark despair of an Almayer or a Decoud. The fatalistic notion that destiny is our absolute master made him endure, perhaps even relish, his isolation. He wrote to Mme. Poradowska:

... solitude loses its terrors when one knows it; it is a tribulation which, for the courageous who have lifted the cup to their lips without flinching, becomes a sweetness whose charm would not be exchanged for anything else in the whole world.[29]

Conrad was bound to be a solitary for, as Marlow believed of a good many people, he was curiously unfitted for the fate awaiting him on this earth. He made a good seaman in spite of his being a romantic dreamer and a son of patriotic Polish landowners. He succeeded as a novelist despite financial hardship, poor health and the problem of writing in English.

This problem was not only that of mastering a foreign language; it also became a moral issue for his compatriots and, eventually, for Conrad himself. Had he been merely a prosperous English captain, occasionally visiting his Polish homeland, the controversy in Poland about the "Polishness" of Conrad and his faithlessness would probably never have arisen. A Pole living abroad was not an uncommon phenomenon and, moreover, when Conrad left his country he was only a youth, under political suspicion from the

Russian authorities. What enraged some of the Polish intellectuals was not Conrad's emigration as such but the fact that it was an emigration of a man of genius, who, they believed, ought to have given his talents to Poland.

The controversy actually began *before* Conrad won wide-spread recognition in England. A Polish philosopher, Wincenty Lutoslawski (author of *Plato's Logic*) wrote two articles entitled "Emigracia Zdolnosci" (The Emigration of Talents) for the St. Petersburg Polish weekly, *Kraj* (Homeland). Lutoslawski claimed that although Conrad's work was published in a foreign language, it was a product of the Polish spirit. He did not blame his compatriot, however, for having left his land. On the contrary, he thought that such emigration of talent could prove beneficial to Poland. At the time of the publication of the article (March, 1899, numbers 12 and 14) this was an exceptional attitude, for even the editors of the moderate and collaborationist *Kraj* would not print the article without an accompanying vehement retort in the same issue of the magazine. Needless to say, the editors identified themselves with the denunciation of Conrad, which was penned by T. Z. Skarszewski, one of the best journalists of the day. The latter preferred a public school teacher in a provincial Polish township to a great man living abroad.

His words are complimentary when compared to the severe censure of the eminent Polish novelist, Mme. Eliza Orzeszkowa (1842–1910), to whom Conrad was a careerist writing popular, lucrative novels in English.

Wrote Mme. Orzeszkowa indignantly in *Kraj* (No. 6, April 16–28, 1899):

And since we talk about books, I must say that the gentleman who is writing novels which are widely read and *bring good profit* almost caused me a nervous attack. When reading about him, I felt something slippery and unpleasant, something mounting to my throat. Really! *That even creative talents should join the exodus!* Till now we have talked only about engineers and operatic singers! But now we should *give absolution to a writer!* As far as chemical or even philosophical works are concerned, I know little about them, and I even perceive some reasons for publishing them sometimes in foreign languages, but because novel writing is attacked, and that's a part of creative production, I belong to the craft, I know the duties *forts comme la mort,* with all my strength—I protest. Creative ability is the very crown of the plant, the very top of the tower, the very heart of the heart of the nation. And to take away from one's nation this flower, this top, this heart and to give it to the Anglo-Saxons who are not even lacking in bird's milk, *for the only reason that they pay better for it one cannot even think of it without shame.* And what is still worse, this gentleman bears the name of his perhaps very near relative,[30] that Joseph Korzeniowski over whose novels I shed as a young girl the first tears of sympathy and felt the first ardors of noble enthusiasms and decisions. Over the novels of Mr. Conrad Korzeniowski no Polish girl will shed an altruistic tear or take a noble decision. But on second thought, this causes me only moderate grief, because believing in the superiority of the elements of which all creative power is composed, I do not suppose that our writers would ever embrace the profession of a vivandiere or a huckster. Besides, we do not starve even if we remain in our place, that we should need to feed on the crumbs from the table of great lords. In this respect we ourselves are *seigneurs* great enough.[31]

Mme. Orzeszkowa could not have been more wrong. Ironically enough, at that time Conrad was struggling against poverty in spite of the good press reviews. Her gloomy predictions about Conrad's future acceptance in Poland did not materialize. Although not always highly popular in Poland, the interest in his work never disappeared, and it recently culminated in what is a veritable revival of the novelist in his native land.

It took Lutoslawski twelve years to reply to Mme. Orzeszkowa's charges. In his book, *Iskierki warszawskie* (Sparks of Warsaw), published in 1911, he tried to explain that had Conrad returned to Poland he would have probably never developed as a writer. Moreover, Conrad's initial success in England stimulated his creative power and helped him become a novelist of stature.

Mme. Orzeszkowa did not merely write an article attacking Conrad. In the white heat of her indignation she wrote him a letter. She must have used some strong words, for Conrad was so hurt that after fifteen years (in the autumn of 1914) he was still furious with her. Said he to Aniela Zagorska, who had urged him to read *Nad Niemnem* (On the Nemen), Eliza Orzeszkowa's outstanding novel, "Bring me nothing by that hag! . . . You don't know, she wrote me such a letter once . . ." [32] Mr. Joseph Ujejski, the well-known Polish critic, who relates this incident, believes that there was a grain of truth in Mme. Orzeszkowa's letter, and it is hard not to reach the conclusion that Conrad himself knew it as well. Had it not been so, he would not have made several attempts to assure his compatriots that he could not write in Polish. These assurances failed to convince them since they were expressed in excellent Polish. Nor should his apologetic manner be easily dismissed as merely a manifestation of Conrad's politeness. He was deeply affected by the accusations of his fellow-Poles. He told his critics that his own literary work in English was unworthy of Polish literature and that he wrote only to earn a living.

In 1896 Lutoslawski went to England and visited Conrad. In reply to Lutoslawski's query why he did not write in Polish Conrad said:

Sir, I hold our beautiful Polish literature in too high esteem to introduce to it my poor writing. But for the English my abilities are sufficient and secure my daily bread.[33]

Reporting on his visit again in 1899 Lutoslawski quoted Conrad as having said:

To write in Polish! That's a great thing, for that one must be a writer like Mickiewicz or Krasinski. I am a common man, I write to earn my living and to support my wife, in the language of the country where I found refuge.[34]

Yet in 1899 Conrad wrote such masterpieces as "Youth" and "Heart of Darkness" and began his *Lord Jim*, which was completed in 1900. A year later Conrad wrote a letter to his namesake, Jozef (Joseph) Korzeniowski who was then director of the Jagiellon Library. The letter, recently obtained by Miss Barbara Kocowna from his family and published in Poland in the 1959 issue of the *Kwartalnik Neofilologiczny* (Neophilological Quarterly), contains a most revealing statement on Conrad's feelings about his "Polishness."

And allow me, Sir, to say here (for it may be that you may hear all sorts of things about me) that I have denied neither my nationality nor our common name for the sake of success. It is clearly known that I am a Pole and that Jozef Konrad are my Christian names of which I use the latter as my last name so that foreign lips should not distort it—which I cannot stand. It doesn't seem to me that I am being unfaithful to my homeland because I have proved to the English that a nobleman [*szlachcic* in Polish—member of the gentry] from the Ukraine can be as good a sailor as they and can have something to say to them in their own language.[35]

In 1920 Conrad asked his cousin for forgiveness because his sons did not speak Polish. Conrad knew the stigma with which he had been branded by his contemporaries for having expatriated himself. It was a painful subject to him in his early years as a writer, and he would speak of it unwillingly.[36]

Jan Lechon, a noted Polish poet (who died tragically in New York in 1956), told me that Stefan Zeromski, the great Polish novelist, once referred to Conrad as "that traitor." But Zeromski wrote a sympathetic preface to the Polish edition of *Lord Jim* and received a rather ingratiating letter from Conrad, thanking him for the honor. The anecdotal information supplied by Lechon sheds light on his own attitude to Conrad, not uncommon among the Polish critics. In his poem entitled, "Na smierc Jozefa Conrada" (On the Death of Joseph Conrad), Lechon speaks more of Conrad's father, who died as a martyr in Poland's struggle for independence, than of Conrad himself.

In 1925 Zeromski restated Conrad's position in Poland. The duty of Polish literature, he wrote, was not to grab an author from the English and make him Polish property, but to bring his spirit to the country by means of excellent translations. He believed, however, that Conrad was as much an English writer as he was a Polish writer. He looked upon him as on "that original spirit, different, new, audacious among our visionaries and writers." These views set a new pattern of critical approach to Conrad. The early hostility toward Conrad soon gave way to a sympathetic consideration of the artist as a great English novelist rather than as guilt-ridden expatriate. But Conrad's Polish heritage still loomed large in most publications. The Polish critics found it difficult to avoid the "'Conrad and Poland" formula, and their essays explored the manifold aspects of this relationship. Conrad's patriotism was scrutinized and questioned; his political views examined, his ties with the Polish tradition investigated. To cite a few early examples: "Jozef Conrad a Polska" (Joseph Conrad and Poland), *Tygodnik Illustrowany*, Nrs. 41–44, pp. 815, 836, 154, 876 (October 10–31, 1925); "Polska w zyciu i dzielach Josepha Conrada (Poland in the life and works of Joseph Conrad), *Droga*, no. 12 (December, 1927), pp. 18–29; "Czy Conrad jest pisarzem polskim?" (Is Conrad a Polish writer?) by Witold Chwalewik, *Mysl Narodowa*, no. 39 (1926), pp. 189–190; no. 40, pp. 208–209; no. 41, pp. 226–228; "Z dziejow J. Conrada Korzeniowskiego w Polsce" (From the history of J. Conrad Korzeniowski in Poland), by Piotr Grzegorczyk, *Ruch Literacki*, no. 2 (May, 1926), pp. 136–138.

The English-speaking critic does not quite appreciate the readiness of the Polish reader to find Polish elements in Conrad's work. What strikes the Pole as an intensely familiar mood of Polish romanticism may appear to the English ear as a merely "exotic" passage, due mainly to Conrad's far voyages. Admittedly, the literary scholar should be wary in his attempt to draw analogies between Conrad's work and that of other writers. But if it is legitimate to discuss his work in relation to Henry James, Melville, Dostoyevsky and Faulkner, why not compare it with the novels of Sienkiewicz, Zeromski and Prus? If the English and the Americans notice allusions to Shakespeare, why not allow allusions to Adam Mickiewicz?

There is little *direct* influence of Polish romantic poetry on Conrad's work, although Professor Ludwik Krzyzanowski was able to point out some remarkable analogies both in the use of language and the description of characters.[31] It is difficult, however, to find many *thematic* analogies since Conrad persistently refrained from writing on Poland (with very rare exceptions). But there is a certain spiritual and moral "atmosphere" in Conrad's work, which brings him close to some Polish masters of literature, particularly when he probes the soul of the strife-torn individual and his relation to society.

A prime example is *Lord Jim*. The sense of mission and the dream of hero leadership, which are largely responsible for Jim's actions, are strikingly similar to those of Mickiewicz's *Konrad Wallenrod*. Conrad, who was named after the hero of this work knew its special connotation in Poland—a symbol of revolt against Russian oppression (even though, to bypass censorship, Mickiewicz substituted the Teutonic Knights of the Cross for Imperial Russia).

Reversing the situation, Julian Krzyzanowski sees in the moral conflict of Konrad Wallenrod, who must use base duplicity and become a traitor so that he may bring defeat to his enemies, a subject which Conrad explored a hundred years later in *Under Western Eyes*. Writing about Mickiewicz's great poem in his *Polish Romantic Literature,* Professor Krzyzanowski shows the analogous conditions of Mickiewicz's time and Conrad's boyhood. He rightly concludes that both the poet and the novelist are concerned with the same issue: the destruction of the human soul by an evil regime.

The relevance of Conrad's themes to the problems of Polish nationhood presents a special appeal to Conrad's Polish readers. The exalted romantic credo of Jim endeared Conrad greatly to the Poles in the dark days of World War II. And when the Conrad centenary was observed in the Western world the Poles did their share to emphasize the importance of Conrad as a great novelist. In December, 1957, the Conrad Centenary celebrations were held in Warsaw. Among the foreign guests who delivered addresses in English were Richard Curle, Conrad's friend and biographer, Jocelyn Baines, one of the editors of Longmans, Green and Co., author of the new biography of Conrad, and Dr. Ivo Vidan of Yugoslavia. The English writers were invited by the Polish Academy of Sciences, the Polish Writers' Union and the Polish PEN Club. The public meetings climaxed what appeared to be a full-scale revival of Conrad in Poland. New editions of Conrad were issued; the leading periodicals in the country printed articles about him, and reviewed the work of American, English and French students of Conrad.

When one recalls that between the years 1950–1955 Conrad was on the blacklist in Stalinist Poland, these celebrations and literary activities assume added significance. They indicate a general liberalization of the official attitude toward the West—a new ideological approach which neither regards Conrad as the misleader of youth nor as a decadent and immoral capitalist writer.

Ironically, in the preface to the 1959 Russian edition of selected stories and novels by Conrad, Mr. N. Bannikov, actually lauds Conrad as a writer opposed to the bourgeois mores. Bannikov thinks highly of Conradian heroes' regard for "comradely solidarity." To quote from the introduction:

The luminous romantic dream of achievement, the sense of duty fill the existence of Conradian heroes, and determine all their actions. The lives of these men, to whom the writer has given his sympathies are a challenge to the middleclass shopkeeping establishments and standards of the bourgeois world, its whole ethics and morality. Conrad praises man's courage and freedom; the decks of the ships he describes are the scenes of a struggle not only against the elements of nature but also against the evil, dark forces of the bourgeois society. Conrad personifies these forces clearly, drawing not a few abominable servants of the golden calf, traitors and scoundrels.

In the pages of his books we find direct or indirect condemnation of the capitalist way of life as well as a profound protest against the enslavement and exploitation of millions of the masses in the East, which are under the heel of white colonizers. He gave expression to a faith that a time would come when those oppressed masses would reveal their richest creative possibilities.

However, Mr. Bannikov hastens to inform the Soviet reader that Conrad has not exactly made the grade as a champion of the cause of "people's democracy"—Communist style. Not all writings of Conrad are "equally valuable and acceptable" to the Soviet public. No mention is made of these offending works. Bannikov merely makes a general statement on the subject:

In some of his works are sounded loud notes of unenlightened fatalism, confusion, unbelief in the future. He did not see the spacious avenues which were opened to mankind by the Great October Revolution in Russia. Yet the attentive reader will feel nonetheless that Joseph Conrad rejected the bourgeois civilization which warps the best qualities of human nature.[38]

The evaluation of Conrad by Poles is a far cry from this

kind of doctrinaire simplification. The Polish critics still admire Conrad, the romantic, but several writers also point to his affinity with the movement which followed on Polish romanticism—positivism, which emphasized hard work, suffering and devotion to duty. One of the recent critics, S. Helsztynski, examines the newly discovered letters of Tadeusz Bobrowski, and stresses the mentorial strictness and stern severity of Bobrowski's guidance. Mr. Helsztynski feels that the positivist philosophy of Conrad's uncle affected the young man's development: it turned him into a model sailor and it is largely responsible for his manly character and the high moral standards of honor. One of the quotations from Bobrowski's letters to Conrad is particularly relevant to this theory since it uses the phrase *usque ad finem,* employed by Stein in a similar context:

I have been through a great deal, I suffered over my own fate, the fate of my family and my nation, and perhaps it is because of these sufferings and disappointments that I developed in myself that calm view of life's task, whose motto, I dare assert, was and is *usque ad finem:* the love of duty perceived in its narrow and wide senses, depending on given circumstances, and therein my practical credo. . . .[39]

This emphatic statement of Conrad's mentor is echoed in Conrad's own pronouncement of his intimate views:

Those who read me know my conviction that the world, the temporal world, rests on a few very simple ideas; so simple that they must be as old as the hills. It rests notably, among others, on the idea of Fidelity.[40]

The articles by S. Helsztynski and W. Chwalewik are the only two writers now living in Poland who have original essays in a Conrad symposium, printed in the 1958 (summer) issue of the *Kwartalnik Neofilologiczny* (Neophilological Quarterly), published by the Polish Academy of Sciences. Out of a total of twenty-four signed entries, ten are devoted to Conrad. Of these, five are written in English by R. Curle, M. C. Bradbrook, J. Baines, I. Vidan and W. Chwalewik. The two articles in Polish are the piece by Helsztynski, "Joseph Conrad—the Man and the Creative Writer," and one by W. Tarnawski, "The Creative Turn of Conrad's Mind and Work." The remaining contributions are a review of Conradian research in Yugoslavia by I. Vidan and two separate reviews by Roza Jablkowska, entitled, "English and American Studies of Conrad," and "Polish Studies of Conrad Abroad."

Mr. Chwalewik's article relates Conrad's work to four major schools of literary art: 1) eighteenth-century humanistic realism (Fielding) 2) nineteenth-century romanticism in poetry 3) late nineteenth-century naturalism 4) the *fin-de-siècle* aestheticism. According to Mr. Chwalewik's thesis, Conrad continues some of the eighteenth century realistic traditions, but he achieves an original synthesis of historically opposed elements, for he is also a romantic at heart. His romanticism, however, derives not from the historical novelists like Walter Scott and Fenimore Cooper but rather from romantic poetry, especially Polish romantic poetry. Conrad disregards the eighteenth-century classical tradition in that he makes no practical distinction between the language of prose and that of poetry, and the tonality of his work resembles the poetry of the so-called Polish-Ukrainian school of the early Polish romantics. The latter looked upon the Podolian "ocean of dry land" as Conrad regarded the vastness of the seas. This school, moreover, stressed some of the themes that are often found in Conrad's work: the romantic concepts of fidelity and honor and the association of great spaces with great silences (e.g., Mickiewicz's *Stepy Akermanskie*, Slowacki's *Lambro*, Malczeski's *Maria*).

Mr. Helsztynski follows the early tradition of Polish Conradiana by being primarily concerned with the novelist's Polish aspects. Mr. Chwalewik goes farther, for he regards Conrad as a modern European novelist, whose work has been influenced by such different writers as Fielding, Mickiewicz, Flaubert, Maupassant, Zola and Rimbaud. Yet though Chwalewik's article sheds some light on the complexity of Conrad's literary heritage, it is, by the author's own admission, merely a sketchy survey of less than nine pages.

Roza Jablkowska, the only other Polish writer of this issue, now working in Poland, evaluates the recent books by Gérard Jean-Aubry, Walter F. Wright, Douglas Hewitt, and Thomas Moser, often citing English and American sources. Somewhat enviously, she discusses the numerous publications on Conrad by émigré writers in the West. One of the poignant items in her commentary on Polish writers abroad is the analysis of Czeslaw Milosz's article, "Joseph Conrad in Polish Eyes," which appeared in the Anniversary issue of *The Atlantic* in 1957. The article is reviewed under eleven headings *(sic)*, the last of which quotes the author's opinions on the Polish ban on Conrad under Stalinist rule. Under heading No. 11 Jablkowska writes, "In the years past Conrad was proclaimed in Poland to be 'an immoral writer, depraving the young.' The main reason for condemning the writer was the fact of his belonging to Western civilization which was then regarded as negative." [41] By implication we may then assume that the present attitude toward the West is quite different from what it was several years ago.

Not all writers in Poland are as qualified as R. Jablkowska. For example, a review of *Vie de Conrad* by Gérard Jean-Aubry, recently published in Poland (known in the U. S. under the title *The Sea Dreamer),* shows either naïveté or simply ignorance of the extensive body of Conrad criticism in the West as well as in Poland. The reviewer, a Mr. Bogdan Wojdowski, demands a definition of "so dramatic a figure as Conrad" and asks for studies of Conrad's prose and historical and sociological comments "on the connections of this cosmopolite [not a Stalinist slip, I hope] with the sundry national and social groupings." We do not know whether this call is addressed to the writers in Poland or to those in the West. The latter have certainly given a fair share of critical commentary on all of these questions.

As a matter of fact, Zdzislaw Najder, a Polish critic and writer, attempts a brief definition of Conrad's philosophy in an article in the *Przeglad Kulturalny* (Cultural Review, December, 1957). The weekly carries an article by M. C. Bradbrook, specially written for the occasion, entitled "Conrad and the Tragic Imagination." It is followed by Najder's piece, called "About the 'Philosophy' of Conrad." Mr. Najder, who appears to be one of the few serious students of Conrad in Poland, discusses the controversy over Conrad in the country, informing us that Jan Kott played the part of the Grand Inquisitor in it. Rather ironically, he dismisses the indictment of Conrad as a decadent novelist. It is obvious that he is familiar with the Western writings on Conrad, from which he occasionally quotes. But he does not bother to give credit to American or English writers when he "discovers" that *Nostromo* is one of Conrad's greatest novels. We are told incidentally, that *Nostromo* is one of the badly translated books of Conrad. Najder is erudite but he is not breaking any really new ground. Conrad's pessimism or, as he puts it, his "tragic optimism," has been amply analyzed in many books and articles by American and English authors.

Mr. Najder does have something interesting to say, however, in another article, "The Three Seasons of Life," in the December, 1957, issue of *Tworczosc* (Creative Work, published in Warsaw, edited by Jaroslaw Iwaszkiewicz). This monthly features a special section on Conrad in honor of the Centenary celebrations. Najder's essay is a well-informed discussion of the major phases of Conrad's creative life. Particularly original is his analogy between Conrad and Czeslaw Milosz.

The hero of the latter's *Siegfried and Erika* shares with Conrad's Kurtz the dream of civilized order. But when he attains power the ideal disappears and only the means of its realization remains. Najder comments on the corruption of extreme power. Kurtz, who wished to eradicate the wilderness, himself turned into an idol of the wilderness, an arch-cannibal, leading one tribe against another. Yet his motives were lofty.

By a strange coincidence the article which follows is a study of Milosz's poetry by Jerzy Kwiatkowski. And, as if this were not enough, Mr. Kwiatkowski suggests that the spirit of Conrad, the writer, pervades the poetry of Milosz, and that both reveal the same kind of moral atmosphere. Conrad certainly had an impact on this issue of the *Tworczosc!*

The Conrad revival in Poland may have had something to do with the new interest in the literary work of his father. For example, The Institute of Literary Studies published a book by R. Taborski, *Apollo Korzeniowski, Ostatni Dramato-pisarz romantyczny* (Apollo Korzeniowski, The Last Romantic Playwright, Warsaw, 1957). This study is listed in the *Biuletyn Polonistyczny* (Polish Bulletin, Warsaw, March, 1958), which also informs us that the Lodz Science Society of Polish Literature is planning to publish in 1959 *Four Studies of Conrad* by Aniela Kowalska, a lecturer in the Department of Polish at the University of Lodz *(Biuletyn Polonistyczny*, Book 2, June, 1958).

On March 29, 1959 the *Tygodnik Powszechny* (Universal Weekly) devoted almost a whole page to "Unknown Letters of Conrad." Two of the three letters printed were submitted to the weekly by Albertyna Cichocka who spent the summer of 1914 with her father and brothers in Zakopane at the boarding house of Mme. Aniela Zagorska, Conrad's cousin. Her daughter (whose name was also Aniela) became the chief translator of Conrad's works into Polish.

The two letters[42] written in 1914 to Cichocka's father,

Stanislaw Zajaczkowski. In her commentary Cichocka relates the circumstances of Conrad's stay in Poland. She describes the friendship between herself, her brother and Conrad's two sons, and she briefly outlines the conditions in Poland after the outbreak of World War I. These letters do not reveal any new information about Conrad's trip to Poland in 1914, but they do offer a good example of his Polish utterance which is idiomatic, free from anglicisms and quite un-literary.

The third letter was written during another Polish visit of Conrad—twenty-four years earlier. It is addressed to Gustaw Sobotkiewicz. In 1890 there were no conditions of stress and sickness to mar his Polish style, which is here adjectival and effusive. The punctuation is rather arbitrary and one sentence is ungrammatical. The phrase, *bede mial szczescie go ogladac* (I shall have the happiness to see you), suggests the English "I shall be happy to see you" rather than the common Polish expression used on a similar occasion. And Conrad's regard for the old man to whom he was writing caused him to use this euphemistic cliché: ". . . the voyage to that last port of life's way, from which one never sails. . . ."

The 1890 letter was found by Maria Kornilowiczowna, who translated Gérard Jean-Aubry's *Vie de Conrad* into Polish. She discovered the letter in Zakopane, among the papers left by a certain Maria Dembowska. Miss Kornilowiczowna tells us that Sobotkiewicz, a distant relative or friend of the Korzeniowskis, participated in the 1863 uprising and after some years of exile in Russia lived in Warsaw. He then settled with his daughter, Maria Bronislawowa Dembowska (whom Conrad mistakenly calls Debowska). The signature in the letter does not seem to be quite clear. It reads K. N. Korzeniowski (the two initials stand for Konrad Nalecz), but the "N" looks more like an "M." However, the date, place, the contents and the tone of the letter make Conrad's authorship undisputed.

Kornilowiczowna draws our attention to a puzzling reference to Pulmann who was the tutor of youthful Conrad. Says Conrad, "He is probably living in Sambir, but I do not know how he is doing." Sambir, of course, was the locale of Conrad's first book, *Almayer's Folly*, a work in progress in the year 1890. Mr. Pulmann could hardly have expected to move to the Malayas from Poland in order to practice medicine. Whether the slip is a simple spelling error or a subconscious identification of Almayer with Pulmann, it presents a fascinating illustration of Conrad's imagination at work. There must have been moments in his life when the border line between the fictitious world of his imagination and the real world of his experience would disappear.

In *A Personal Record* Conrad speaks of Pulmann's decision to enter upon medical studies, shortly after the European tour which they took together. Conrad describes how he learned of his tutor's death:

A day came when, on the deck of a ship moored in Calcutta, I opened a letter telling me of the end of an enviable existence. He had made for himself a practice in some obscure little town of Austrian Galicia. And the letter went on to tell me how all the bereaved poor of the district, Christians and Jews alike, had mobbed the good doctor's coffin with sobs and lamentations at the very gate of the cemetery.

How short his years and how clear his vision! What greater reward in ambition, honor and conscience could be have hoped to win for himself when, on the top of the Furca Pass, he bade me look well to the end of my opening life.[43]

The little town in Galicia was probably Sambor. And the two men, Pulmann and Almayer, had one important thing in common: they produced an impact on Conrad's imagination. The former guided his early thought, while the latter stirred the incipient novelist in Captain Joseph Korzeniowski. One is left wondering, as one reads Conrad's letter to Sobotkiewicz, to what extent his mind was preoccupied with the vision of Almayer and his grandiose schemes, as he reminisced nostalgically of the old times in March of 1890.

In a different kind of reminiscence the noted Polish writer, Maria Dabrowska, spoke of the meaning of Conrad to her. The March, 1959 issue of *Nowa Kultura* (The New Culture, No. 21,/478/) published her article "Pozegnanie z Conradem" (A Farewell to Conrad). Although Dabrowska is not a Conradian scholar, her remarks are interesting and often incisive. Thus, for example, she observes that the Polish title of *Chance* should not be *Los* but rather *Traf* which is far more accurate. Also, she feels that *Wykole-jeniec* is hardly the equivalent of *Outcast*, and suggests that the correct Polish title of *An Outcast of the Islands* ought to be *Wygnaniec z wysp* or *Wygnany z wysp*. Joseph Ujej-ski preferred the word *Wyrzutek*. It seems that some Polish translators take undue liberties with the titles of Conrad's works. Another instance is Jessie Conrad's book, *Joseph Conrad and His Circle*. The Polish edition appeared under the title *Joseph Conrad*. This, Dabrowska says, is wrong, for the novelist's circle *is* the substance of the book.

Conrad once expressed his extreme annoyance with the quality of the Polish translations of his works. In 1914 (several months before his trip to Poland) Conrad was asked by Marian Dabrowski, a Polish journalist, whether he liked the Polish versions of his works. He burst out:

Oh, no! I have never been asked for my permission to have them translated, and they are, moreover, so badly translated into Polish. It is a veritable torture for me to read in my native tongue a thing written in English. For I know Polish and French well. And the Polish translations are so careless, so dishonest in their relation to the contents. While the French translations are faultless, the Polish ones will always irritate me. Take, for example, this excerpt in the Lwow journal. Awful, simply awful! Even the word "Malay" was translated as "little Negro." . . .[44]

During the years that followed many works of Conrad were admirably rendered into Polish, especially those translated by his cousin, Aniela Zagorska, whose labors have been hailed as a genuine contribution to Polish literature.

Dabrowska is irritated by the afterword to the Polish version of *Chance* (the translator's name is not mentioned), which states that Conrad "took a lively interest in Polish problems, as reflected in the themes of his creative work and his interests (e.g., the Napoleonic epoch)." Conrad's interest in Napoleon, Dabrowska asserts, had nothing to do with the Polish question. Conrad hated Napoleon, whose "caesarism" he considered as the inevitable outcome of every revolution. The afterword also informs the reader that "the mechanism and the laws governing the capitalist world were not fully perceived by the writer [Conrad] who, having behind him so many excellent sea novels, for the first time attempted this difficult and many-sided theme." Dabrowska points out that when Conrad was writing *Chance* he had already composed "Heart of Darkness," "An Outpost of Progress" and *Nostromo*. And, we might add, also *Lord Jim, The Secret Agent* and *Under Western Eyes!* Moreover, the Polish reader is told that "Conrad's novels constitute a new, splendid chapter in the history of marine literature." To which Dabrowska indignantly retorts: "Conrad would have turned in his grave had he heard those words."

Maria Dabrowska's renewed acquaintance with Conrad after a period of 45 years was not limited to the reading of *Chance*, begun in 1914, but it was not too extensive either. In fact, most of her ideas about him stem from the reading of the following volumes: Gérard Jean-Aubry, *Vie de Conrad*, Jessie Conrad, *Joseph Conrad and His Circle*, the London symposium *Conrad zywy* (The Living Conrad)[45] and Joseph Ujejski, *O Konradzie Korzeniowskim* (About Conrad Korzeniowski). Dabrowska's analysis of Conrad's creative pains is old hat, and her defense of Jessie Conrad as a writer is not particularly rewarding. It is obvious that she sympathizes deeply with Conrad's wife and disagrees with Roza Jablkowska's foreword to Jessie's book, in which she cites the uncomplimentary opinions of Graham Greene and H. L. Mencken. Although she admits that Jablkowska is trying to do justice to the personality of Jessie Conrad, her censure of Jessie's triviality, snobbery and lack of intelligence is too severe. Dabrowska does not find any self-pity or pettiness in Jessie's book. On the contrary, she feels that Conrad's wife portrays well the difficulties of living with a man of genius. And, she hastens to add, Jessie does have a sense of humor, even though she herself assures the reader of it. It appears that Dabrowska echoes a similar defense of Jessie by the Polish translator of her book, Wanda Nalecz-Korzeniowska who wrote the preface.

What appeals to Dabrowska most is Jessie Conrad's portrait of "a foreigner in England" who has never lost his "inner Polishness"—a man marked by a paradoxical dichotomy of character. If Conrad was a true Polish patriot, as so many Polish critics claimed him to be, his was indeed a strange kind of nationalism, for "he could not be held within his own nationality, he adopted another one, and considered 'national egoism' repulsive." His duality can also be seen in his intense dislike of socialism although his best life-long friends looked favorably upon it.

Maria Dabrowska reviews the essays in *Conrad zywy*, stating her preferences but not advancing any new theories. She concludes with a suggestion that perhaps it is more important to study Conrad's influence on other writers than to probe the sundry literary influences on his artistic development. However, she does not live up to her stimulating proposition except for her confession that she herself was influenced by Conrad. Thus, she recalls having penned the following note in the margin of Joseph Ujejski's study of the novelist: "Not with Proust but with Conrad began the writer's struggle to break the conventions of the novel."

She also admits that the scene between Bogumil and Katelba in the beginning of the third volume of her outstanding novel, *Noce i dnie* (Nights and Days), "is not without Conrad's influence."

Through the drama of Conrad, Dabrowska feels, "the best men on both sides" could engage in "long, nocturnal conversations of neighbors." The most vital thing about the contacts between the Polish critics of Conrad in Poland and those abroad is "the real victory over mutual stereotypes of emotion, thought and action." With this she proposes to end "[my] divagations and thereby [my] active contact with the writer, which for many years was an important 'adventure of my soul.'"

The article by Maria Dabrowska also appeared as the concluding essay in an anthology of her writings entitled *Sketches about Conrad,* published in Warsaw in 1959.[46] The reviews and essays in this book date back to the year 1924 and deal with a variety of topics, e.g., "Conrad's Concept of Reality" (1929), "Social and Religious Elements in Conrad's Works" (1932), "Tragedy in Conrad" (1925), and "Conrad's Concept of Fidelity" (1946). To this Polish novelist and critic Conrad is neither an offender against Marxist ideology (as Jan Kott charged),[47] nor a traitor to nationalist morality. She regards him as a man who was faithful to himself as well as to his homeland. What especially appeals to the Polish reader is the quality of affirmation in Conrad's fiction. The Poles find solace in reading Conrad because even in his tragic novels, where evil triumphs irrevocably, he does not deny the possibility of seeking and of finding a meaning in life, albeit this meaning is often limited to the hero's sense of duty toward his work and toward his fellow men.

It is little wonder that the scope of Conradian research in Poland is modest. The six years of Nazi occupation were not conducive to literary studies of the writer, although he was read avidly; nor were the labor camps in Siberia (for many thousands of Poles) any better; nor the Soviet occupation. Poland suffered a frightful toll in intellectual life. During the post-war period no new editions of Conrad were printed, and it culminated in his being blacklisted. Since 1955, however, distinct changes have taken place. The general tone of the major literary publications in the country is a far cry from the witch-hunting hysteria of its Eastern neighbor, directed against Boris Pasternak. Perhaps a Polish version of *Doctor Zhivago* could also run into publication problems; it is doubtful whether its author would be violently denounced and ostracized, for some openly anti-Communist émigré writers have been reviewed and even published in Poland during the past few years. We may hope, therefore, that the present interest in Joseph Conrad will yet bring us important insights into the novelist's work from Poland's critics—that is, if the Stalinists do not return to power and once more pronounce upon Conrad the merciless verdict of Socialist realism.

It would be most erroneous to assume that the Polish view of Conrad is limited to work done in Poland. The startling fact is (at the moment at any rate) that Polish writers living outside their homeland manifest an equal if not greater interest in the life and work of Joseph Conrad, and that their output is quite impressive. The Union of Polish Writers Abroad celebrated the centenary of Conrad's birth in an anthology called *Conrad zywy* (The Living Conrad), published in London in 1957.[48] This collective volume is a revaluation of certain aspects of Conrad from the Polish view. Of the three sections in the book (literary, critical and documentary-historical), only the latter two contain significant critical material. They deal, among others, with a detailed description of Conrad's home country, with Conrad's political stereotypes and his relation to the literary movement of "Young Poland." The problem of dual nationality is explored; Conrad's attitude to Dostoyevsky, Tolstoy and Turgenev is discussed; his father's letters are studied. "The Rescuer" manuscript and *An Outcast of the Islands* are given a new analytical treatment. The first draft of *Lord Jim* and Conrad's Polish letters in American collections are reviewed; eighteen unpublished letters from Joseph Conrad to John Galsworthy are printed and, finally, Conrad's position among Polish people at home and abroad is appraised by several writers. Most of the critics represented in *The Living Conrad* reside in England, but some make their homes in France, the United States and Switzerland; two writers from Poland are also included.

An American version of *The Living Conrad* has been published this year by the Polish Institute of Arts and Sciences under the title *Joseph Conrad: Centennial Essays,* edited by Ludwik Krzyzanowski, who also edits *The Polish Review* and is a serious Conradian scholar himself.

The extraordinary interest in Conrad's Polish heritage is perfectly legitimate criticism, and it is not a recent thing, of course. Gustav Morf's study of the subject[49] in 1930 was perhaps the first serious attempt to relate Conrad's work to his Polish background. However, it also proved that unless the critic exercises caution and prudence in his method he runs the risk of blinding biographical infatuation. Morf's thesis is ingenious and quite penetrating but, unfortunately, he sometimes reaches conclusions which are supported only by his passion for simplification. A random example will illustrate the pitfalls facing the biographical psychoanalyst.

To Morf *Lord Jim* is, from beginning to end, a subconscious confession of treason by Conrad. He considers the name of the ship in the novel, the *Patna,* to be a misspelling of the Polish name for Poland, *Polska.* Hence, Jim's leap from the *Patna* is the equivalent of Conrad's "jump" from Poland into British allegiance. Morf ignores the fact that it took Conrad a good many years to make up his mind on the matter, for it may interfere with the smooth symbolism he expounds. The French gunboat that tows the luckless ship to Aden is not simply a ship. It is the symbol of Polish hope for the salvation of their country by the friendly French, and so on and so forth.

No one can disagree with Morf when he points out how the loneliness of Conrad resembles the condition of his protagonists. But it is a mistake to explain and explain away the complexities of Conrad's characters by means of a total identification of his heritage as a Pole with the various lives of his heroes. Jim is *not* a typical Pole (as Morf fondly wants him to be), nor are his problems invariably bound up with Conrad's feeling of guilt. Jim is not all Conrad, the Pole. Surely, in the analysis of Conrad, the man and the artist, the twenty years of sea life and the similarly long period of the writing years ought to be as important factors as was his departure from Poland at the age of seventeen.

Some critics have gone to the other extreme. Ignoring Conrad's past, his extensive reading, the complexity of his perception, his interest in psychology and ethics, they saw in him only a writer of sea stories. Conrad resented this attitude, insisting that his interests were terrestrial, after all. He claimed that the "sea stuff" in his fiction served a special purpose, on which he elaborated in his Prefaces. He did not think that the presence of seamen in a good many of his books made them sea stories. He stated his point clearly in a letter to Richard Curle (dated July 14, 1923), in which he hoped for an opportunity

. . . to get freed from that infernal tail of ships and that obsession of my sea life, which has about as much bearing on my literary existence, on my quality as a writer, as the enumeration of drawing rooms which Thackeray frequented could have had on his gift as a great novelist. After all, I may have been a seaman, but I am a writer of prose. Indeed, *the nature of my writing runs the risk of being obscured by the nature of my material.*[50]

But, of course, many of Conrad's books *are* an eloquent tribute to life at sea and an expression of "unalterable and profound affection for the ships, the seamen, the winds and the great sea," which were "the moulders of [my] youth, the companions of the best years of my life." [51] Like Proust, he turned to his memories of the past (mostly seafaring), which he recaptured with a feeling of special piety. He often spoke of the influence of his sea training on his character and noted the fact that it was not good equipment for a literary life. But he also observed that everything could be found at sea, as in the pursuit of literature. Such contradictory utterances are frequently found in his works of fiction and memoirs. But then, although Conrad was one of the most conscientious artists that ever lived, he rarely followed a consistent literary theory, relying for the most part on his impulses. His artistic logic obeyed the unpredictable dictates of his temperament.

When the biographical method becomes a psychoanalysis of the writer, with his books rather than himself laid on the psychoanalyst's couch, it is fraught with grave danger of exaggeration (as Mr. Morf's study amply demonstrates). However, this method is quite sound if it is tempered with caution and common sense. In Conrad's case it seems most appropriate. The isolatoes of his novels and stories are, in many a sense, avatars of Conrad's own life. An exile from his country, persistently pursued by ill-health and misfortune, melancholy by temperament, Conrad was an isolato *par excellence.*

We may safely discard his occasional dislike of the connection between his work and his experiences at sea, or in Poland, and accept his own claim that

. . . a novelist lives in his work. He stands there, the only reality in an invented world, among imaginary things, happenings and people. Writing about them, he is only writing about himself. But the disclosure is not complete. He remains, to a certain extent, a figure behind the veil. [52]

How could it be otherwise? Consider the sadness of his childhood, the hardships of his sea years and the agony of his writing career. Each of these three phases of his life tended to enhance Conrad's inborn trait of melancholy. Like his suffering protagonists Lord Jim, Lingard, Captain Whalley, Emilia Gould, Lena, Nostromo, Decoud, Heyst and many others, he felt that loneliness was

. . . a hard and absolute condition of existence; the envelope of flesh and blood on which our eyes are fixed melts before the out-stretched hand, and there remains only the capricious, unconsolable, and elusive spirit that no eye can follow, no hand can grasp.[53]

Indeed, this was a well-known condition to Conrad, as he struggled against poverty or illness and also against the frightening paralysis of expression. Often he resented his profession bitterly, and his complaints about the hardships of the writer fill a sizable volume. He experienced moments of mental blankness, and at times it was a feeling of sheer physical exhaustion as a result of working strain. It was also the ever-present fear of the future, for his profits were not adequate. "There is neither inspiration nor hope in my work," he wrote, "it's mere hard labor for life."[54]

Even after some of his masterpieces had been completed and accepted by the critics as such, Conrad still suffered from his sense of isolation. For example, in 1903, with Lord Jim, "Youth" and "Heart of Darkness" behind him, Conrad thus described his mental condition:

I feel myself strangely growing into a sort of *Outcast, a mental and moral Outcast*. I hear nothing—think of nothing—I reflect nothing—*I cut myself off*—and with all that can just only keep going, or rather keep on lagging from one wretched story to another—and always deeper in the mire.[55]

Conrad accomplished his artistic aims at the cost of a lifetime of suffering and somewhere in the process he came to doubt there were ethical aims in life. Was life then, as he suggested, purely spectacular? Was brute existence its sole purpose? Could man's acts, ideas and emotions be ends in themselves?

Even if it were so, Conrad's fiction suggests, life should not be an object of despair. Hence, the failure and the futility of man's efforts are not necessarily defeat. On the contrary, defeat may sometimes be an affirmation of the ideal value of things. This basic idealism of Conrad and his notion of fidelity, with which he was imbued in his childhood and at sea, helped him become a great master of the English novel. He carried the sailor's concept of duty aboard a ship into the field of letters, regarding himself as a slave of the writers' galley, where, chained voluntarily, he labored with a scrupulous, unflagging perseverance. Having isolated himself as an artist, he unfolded his particular vision of humanity, looking at it and at himself with the perfect detachment of distance. It is to this Olympian isolation of Conrad that we owe the inimitable portrait of man struggling against terrific powers—the forces of nature, destiny, or a morbid obsession with an idea.

This picture of the solitary individual is often a dramatization of Conrad's own misery, of the conflict in him between duty and self-pity, the conflict between the idle dreamer and the man of action. It also indicates Conrad's preoccupation with a *motif* which is recurrent in modern literature. It is the familiar theme of man's insufficiency, alienation and guilt.

CHAPTER **II**

TO FOLLOW THE DREAM

THE ROMANTIC MAN is condemned to isolation by the nature of his endeavor, which is to view life through the prism of his personal illusion. The various elements of the universe, the real and the ideal, the natural and the supernatural, are fused by the power of his imagination into a dream which he will pursue relentlessly and with little thought about the possible consequences of his actions. He is a possessed man who recognizes but one kind of reality—that of his imagination, of his personal belief.

Only a few of Conrad's characters find the substance of the romantic dream to be a sustaining power. To most of them it is a very destructive element. Let us first examine some of the people in Conrad's fiction, to whom an illusion makes life worthwhile even when it is painfully isolated. An interesting example of this situation can be found in "Heart of Darkness," whose main protagonist is killed by *his* particular dream. Marlow has come back from the Congo, bringing the news of Kurtz's death to his fiancée. The girl wishes to know what his last words were, but Marlow is too humane to tell her the truth. He cannot shock the poor creature with a true account of Kurtz's moral and physical deterioration. Compassionately, he lies to her, telling her that Kurtz died with the name of his Intended on his lips. This is a far cry from the words, "The horror! The horror!" which Kurtz actually pronounced, but it is exactly what the lonely woman has expected to hear. Marlow is struck by a sense of unreality at her capacity for suffering and fidelity, the same feeling he experienced when he listened to the lengthy and mad discourse of Kurtz in the wilderness of the Congo. Kurtz was utterly alone with his dream, and so was this unfortunate woman with her memory of him, which she wanted to preserve for the rest of her life. She needs to be reassured in her faith in Kurtz, but even if Marlow had not lied to her, she would have refused to believe the truth. Ironically, the truth does not matter as long as her faith remains intact—"that great and saving illusion that shone with an unearthly glow in the darkness." [1]

Another character in "Heart of Darkness" thrives on the substance of his dream—the be-patched Russian youth who displays a delightful naïveté in the midst of a grim wilderness. This ragged young man is totally unaware of his apparent destitution and loneliness. His thoughtless audacity makes him indestructible. He can toy with death because it is meaningless to him. He treads the earth, imbued with "the absolutely pure, uncalculating, unpractical spirit of adventure." [2]

Similarly, young Marlow in "Youth" is incapable of seeing things in their true perspective, refusing to acknowledge the realities of sea life. The hardships and the dangers of a shipwreck (which are anything but glamor to the ordinary sailor) are to him the most glorious manifestations of adventure, the best time of his life. He has been touched by "that great and saving illusion."

Whatever the result of a dream may be, it eventually reveals the fundamental discrepancy between illusion and reality. An older dreamer, like Stein, recognizes the appalling incongruity of life—that man's dreams may not be attained, and yet he must forever dream. Stein is also a realist in being able to understand the true nature of romantic dreams. He knows that reality must close down inexorably upon man, and the dream may turn into a destructive nightmare, but the realist gives in to the romantic.

What makes a romantic dream lose its appeal and change into a nightmare is primarily its paralyzing power. Lord Jim and the Lingard of *The Rescue* are unable to act in the most crucial moments of their lives. Although Lingard does not experience Jim's inability to act as a result of psychic identification with another person (since neither Mrs. Travers nor her husband can take Brown's place), his nature is as romantic as Jim's. In his acts

. . . performed simply, from conviction, what may be called *the romantic side of the man's nature* came out; *that responsive sensitiveness to the shadowy appeals made by life and death* which is the groundwork of a chivalrous character.[3]

This sensitiveness was Conrad's at the beginning of his writing career. This is how he felt in October, 1899:

The unreality of it [of writing for a living] seems to enter one's real life, penetrating into the bones, make the very heart beats *pulsate illusions* through the arteries. One's will becomes *the slave of hallucinations, responds only to shadowy impulses,* waits on imagination alone, a strange state, a trying experience, a kind of *fiery trial of untruthfulness.* And one goes through it,—there's nothing to show at the end. Nothing! Nothing! Nothing![4]

Fortunately for us, Conrad was wrong about producing nothing at the end. He was paralyzed by his dreams only in the sense of being temporarily checked in the task of literary composition, but the secret of his appeal often rests with his artistic responsiveness to the "shadowy impulses" of his imagination.

The conflict between passion and honor was in Conrad already when he decided to go to sea. The unreality of a writer's life, no less than his previous experiences, further enhanced it. The mature novelist did not transfer this inner conflict upon his heroes in an autobiographical fashion. Only the sentiment of the author remains unchanged. Actually, in Jim's case honor is the passion itself. Jim does not really love Jewel, and it is her love for him that is thwarted by his determination to have his good name, and to pay the debt of honor. Unlike Mrs. Travers, Jewel is totally powerless before Jim's tacit verdict against himself. He has freed himself from any bonds except those of his own will, thus emerging as a stronger man than the masterful Lingard. The dream of achievement and an exalted faith in their own powers are common to both men, and neither has the full understanding of the latent weakness in his nature. Jim's moment of indecision and cowardice proves his undoing. Lingard's sudden, consuming passion for a woman brings him to the brink of destruction. Both men are failures. For all his success in Patusan and his freedom to choose between life and death, Jim's original vision of himself as the hero of the seas has not come true; nor has Lingard fared better at the hands of Destiny that interferes with his schemes. The romantic ideal has set these two men apart from their fellow beings, and it has led to ruin rather than to glory.

Conrad's books dealing with the life of Lingard (in reverse chronological order: *Almayer's Folly, An Outcast of the Islands, The Rescue*) and *Lord Jim* illustrate his belief that man carries the seeds of self-destruction in his own soul. Tom Lingard, significantly described as "the descendant of the immortal hidalgo errant upon the sea," [5] is a victim of his own impulses. His insatiable ambition to act as the benevolent despot, and his chivalrous tenderness toward women were bound to result in disaster even had there been no tragedy of accident and error. In all the

books describing him he moves within the glamor of a lawless life, "very lonely, dangerous and romantic." [6]

The story of the unfortunate rescue is less a tale of
adventure than an account of a conflict—a moral issue posed
before Tom Lingard by the unpredictable appearance of
Mr. Travers' yacht in "his" waters, and by his subsequent
love for Mrs. Travers. His loyalty to Hassim (an exiled
Malayan prince who had saved his life, and whose kingdom
he now attempts to restore) clashes with his feeling of duty
towards the party of the whites, and his concern with the
fate of Edith Travers. The conflict is clearly defined by
the title of Part V, "the Point of Honor and the Point of
Passion."

Lingard's honor and his reputation among the natives
are at stake. Honor, Lingard declares, is "something a man
needs to draw free breath." [7] D'Alcacer agrees with him,
amiably advising him to recognize another important thing
a man needs—humanity. Lingard's good name cannot be
reconciled with the defence of the whites. His passion for
Mrs. Travers immensely complicates the situation. Even if
there had been some way out of the crisis, it is doubtful
whether Lingard would have been able to follow it, for
his romantic love has caused him to lose his power of
thought and action. His illusioned vision of Edith Travers
and himself as partners proves fatal. It makes him forfeit
his grip on reality and it is as paralyzing as Jim's picture
of himself in danger and his self-probing restlessness. He
becomes

. . . a stranger to all men, and abandoned by the All-knowing
God. . . .

The fierce power of his personality seemed to have turned
into a dream.[8]

Mrs. Travers also falls under the spell of an illusion.
She has led a brilliant life, but she has not known the
meaning of sincerity or true passion. She has not experi-

enced a single true emotion. That is why she is so easily
fascinated by Lingard and his savage friends who live in a
different world. She envies the lot of the unhappy exiled
princess because the girl could afford to be candid and
courageous and had no need to hide her feelings. Edith's
imagination was captured by this simplicity of character.
In this new world one could be tender and passionate and
ferocious. Lingard ruled it. As the romantic dreams of her
childhood came back to her, he suddenly appeared to be
the embodiment of a great passion. His strength and mag-
nanimity stirred in her unknown impulses. The temptation
to surrender to the Man of Fate was enhanced by the
wilderness which surrounded them all, and which, in Conrad's work, is always a symbol of moral corruption.

There is more interesting symbolism in the book. Lingard is waiting in the besieged stockade for Mrs. Travers.
On her way to meet him she drops her veil. This is her
symbolic manifestation of surrender to her dream of a great
passion. Lingard believes that she has come for his sake
alone. When he crushes her in his powerful embrace, lift-
ing her off the ground, Mrs. Travers loses one of her san-
dals, which signifies her partial loss of touch with the reality
of the world of her common experience. For a short moment
it seems that hers is a submission that comes from love.
Lingard believes that she has risked her life in order to
come to him; this thought makes him lose his head completely. A man in this state of mind could not have thought
of asking the simple question: "Have you any message for
me?" He thus made it easier for Mrs. Travers to conceal
the truth. If there had been a momentary impulse in her
to yield to the temptation, there were at least two strong
factors acting against it: her devotion to Mr. Travers and
a half-conscious realization, later made obvious to her, that
Lingard had no place in the social organization of which
she was part.

The dream had indeed turned into a nightmare. Lingard's romantic figure appeared to her in sleep as a sinister image in armor, resembling a Crusader. She replaced her lost sandal, and thus restored the contact with the earth—with the realities of life. She found her lost veil and thus once again donned the mask of civilization. The spell simply did not work. She may have been disloyal to Mr. Travers' ideal of respectability, but she could not lose herself in her dream as Lingard did in his. At the end of their affair she could only shamefacedly admit to him that she shuddered at the thought of meeting him again. She came to see him on the lonely sandbank in order to make her confession and because *he* had all the right on his side. She came to pay her debts to the uttermost farthing, as her moral code required. She wanted to avoid future remorse. In a sense, she felt humiliated and wished to be punished by this masterful adventurer, so that she might expiate her lie about the ring. When she realized he knew of her falsehood, she passionately asked to be thrown into the sea. Perhaps she was ready to receive punishment at his hands. What she could not do, however, was to remain with Lingard as his mistress or wife. Only now he began to understand that she had been an illusion to him, but so forceful an illusion that he would be unable to shed it for the rest of his life.

As the two lovers confront each other on a small and deserted island, the only people in the open ocean, their awful solitude is revealed to them. They have nothing in common with each other. For the first time Lingard can see Mrs. Travers as she really is. His dream has been shattered. Edith is made of too hard a clay. The man of "infinite illusions" has paid the price of "the romantic necessity that had invaded his life." [9] Mrs. Travers, too, has to pay the penalty for the encounter with Lingard. Her predilection for extreme opinions and exotic costumes, her sympathy with the lawless characters and romantic personalities, have brought out her separateness more acutely.

She felt strongly *her isolation.* She was so much the only being of her kind moving within this mystery that even to herself she looked like an apparition without rights and without defense. . . . Hers was *the most complete loneliness,* charged with a catastrophic tension. It lay about her as though she had been *set apart within a magic circle.*[10]

Although she now sees Mr. Travers as a dull and silly creature, Edith cannot leave her husband. As their ship sails away, leaving behind the broken-hearted Lingard, she flings overboard the symbolic ring which she failed to deliver. It is now a dead talisman.

In the autobiographical *The Arrow of Gold,* George is a variation on the theme of Lingard. The circumstances of their respective crises are quite different, of course, but there are many points of similarity. Lingard risks and loses his reputation, trying to protect a group of white people with whom he has nothing in common, and for whom he has little regard. George risks his life in a Carlist adventure although its cause means nothing to him. When he returns from his escapade he experiences the state of mind with which Lingard was familiar at the end of his affair. This is how young George describes his emotions:

Nothing could have marked better *my status of a stranger, the completest possible stranger in the moral region* in which those people lived, moved, enjoying or suffering their incomprehensible emotions. *I was as much of a stranger as the most hopeless castaway* stumbling in the dark upon a hut of natives and finding them in the grip of some situation appertaining to the mentalities, prejudices, and problems of an undiscovered country—of which he had not even had a single clear glimpse before. . . .[11]

Both men suffer the pangs of a passionate love which deprives them of their power of sound judgment and completely shakes their moral equilibrium. George's passion is like a sickness. It makes him lose his hold on the world, blurring his conception of reality, wreaking destruction in his soul. The memory of Rita's laughter, the true memory of the senses, seems to him more penetrating than reality itself. At times Rita is to him merely a cold illusion. At times she is a searing flame within him, which consumes his body and mind. In his love for her, George claims that she exists in him only. Like Lingard, he can see her clearly when she is gone, and he too will be haunted by her image after the affair is over.

Rita is also a haunted creature and a pariah despite her wealth and beauty. When a loathsome admirer points out to her that she owns four houses, his words make her feel *"a homeless outcast* more than ever—like a little dog lost in the street—not knowing where to go." [12] The trouble with Rita, as with Lingard, Lord Jim and other romantics of Conrad, is her extraordinary sensibility which creates for her a moral problem where another person would see none. She is skeptical about her life's ethics. "As to my living . . . acting, working wonders at a little cost . . . it has all but killed me morally." [13] Rita is not of this world. Being different from other women, she is puzzled by her own personality, from which she unsuccessfully attempts to escape. In George's words, her life seems to be a continuous running away. Surrounded by a host of men who desire her, respect her and envy her, she is painfully alone. Rita's maid repeatedly assures George that Madame has no friend, intimating that he is the only one who could make her mistress happy. Their happiness, however, cannot be more than a brief spell.

The love-nest of Rita and George is a paradise of isolation. A thick veil of secrecy is suspended between the world and the two lovers. No longer separated from each other, they now share a "perfect detachment from all mundane affairs." [14] "This world," Mills remonstrates gently, "is not a world of lovers, not even for such lovers as *you two who have nothing to do* with the world as it is." [15] The world, in other words, does not permit an escape from all mundane affairs. The love of George and Rita cannot be consummated unless they live in total seclusion from the outside world. And since Doña Rita realizes, as Mills does, that a world of lovers would be impossible, she flees from what is dearest to her, heroically sacrificing herself to the integrity of George's life, thus giving him the supreme proof of her love.

An integral life, to George, cannot be an existence of love alone, for he must also live as a seaman. Rita understands that a young fellow of nineteen without fortune or position ought not to be chained to her by his passion. Therefore she leaves him after the duel which he fights for her honor. George is hurt by what he believes to be a desertion, forgetting that as a pigheaded enthusiast of the sea he will not lose that other love of his—the ships and the dream of adventure.

Rita is far more unfortunate, for she cannot return to her goats and poverty. She has been admired, adored, persecuted and now she has had her moment of happiness. But she knows that she cannot let George wage duels on her behalf for the rest of their lives. Perhaps, Mills remarks philosophically, she may find something in life. Yet it will be neither love nor peace—the things she wanted most. Like most women of Conrad, she has no real place in her man's life; she is outside his main passion—the sea.

The impact of sudden disaster on a man is a recurrent means in Conrad's work for isolating the individual from his environment or for alienating him from another human being he loves. The dream of life, like other dreams, can be shattered by an unexpected blow of fate. But adverse circumstances are only partly responsible for the failure to attain consummation in love. The fault is often with the lovers themselves, who are incapable of true understanding. Thus, the calamity which besets them is only an outward agent that triggers off the inevitable rift between them. Heemskirk in "Freya of the Seven Isles" is such an agent, an epitome of evil; and Freya, like Rita de Lastaola, is the object of his malicious persecution. Unable to win her love, Heemskirk vengefully destroys the chance of happiness that Freya may have had with Jasper Allen, by taking Jasper's brig away from him.

Upon a closer analysis of the characters, however, we are no longer certain whether Jasper Allen and Freya could really have been happy together under *any* circumstances. Heemskirk's wickedness would have been of no avail had Freya and Allen been free from selfishness. To the girl her freedom means more than her lover—at any rate before the tragedy strikes. To Jasper his brig is more precious than his life. Without his ship he dare not face the world, and he deteriorates morally and physically. He turns into a beachcomber who wanders aimlessly along the shore, staring at his stranded brig, which, like a symbol of despair, towers above the lonely sea-horizon. Freya dies of loneliness and remorse, after admitting that she has been conceited, headstrong and capricious. She has sought her own gratification and not a happy union with Jasper. Freya's end supports Marlow's belief (in *Chance*) that the germ of destruction lies in wait for man, even at the very source of his strength.

The strong will of Doña Erminia in "Gaspar Ruiz" is responsible for her death. She will not surrender to the new government forces on whom she wants to take revenge, and she uses Gaspar Ruiz as a mere tool to further her goal. She does not bother to come close to her husband until it is too late. When Gaspar Ruiz lies on the ground with his back broken Erminia realizes her affection for him. The intensity of her hate has blotted out every other sentiment from her heart.

The concentration on a single idea or purpose at times turns into a ludicrous mania (Mrs. Fyne in *Chance*) or into a murderous rage (Mrs. Winnie Verloc in *Under Western*

Eyes). The loss of a proper balance of emotions is invariably punished. To some extent, Conrad's negation of the "independent" woman by ridiculing the masculine type is Victorian. Mostly, however, his vision of women is romantic.

Freya and Erminia belong to that group of Conrad's women which does not conform to *his* idea of womanhood. Most of his women are not concerned with earning for themselves a place in society. They very seldom challenge destiny. They are passive, and this, Conrad hastens to add in Flora de Barral's case, does not mean inanimate, for they may put up an appearance of agitation. Marlow believes that women must needs wait on fate. Any hesitation to accept this statement as Conrad's own view is discarded when we study his heroines in the novels and stories. We find a predominance of the "passive" type and a rich variety of enigmatic, immobile and silent women who, like their male counterparts, have one thing in common: their isolation. The verdicts of destiny do not distinguish between the "real" passive women and the headstrong type. The former are also hapless and helpless victims, as Flora's lot shows, perhaps more pathetic because of the feebleness of their efforts to oppose destruction.

Forsaken and insulted by her vicious governess after her father's bankruptcy, Flora experiences a profound moral shock. This betrayal alone would endanger the mental state of an average girl. But for Flora this is only the beginning of her sufferings. She must live among her relatives, a passive, persecuted victim. Her fortunes do not take a better turn when she runs away to the Fynes. Her father being in jail, she is a social outcast with no friends and no occupation to turn her mind away from the contemplation of her own misery and worthlessness. She has an acute inferiority complex.

The abuse of the governess left a mark on Flora's soul, "a sort of *a mystic wound*, to be contemplated, to be meditated over." [16] Like Jim, she keeps harping on the past even when, to all intents and purposes, a chance has been given her to forget it. Marlow's contention that Flora was the most forlorn damsel of modern times is quite right. She is described as being detached, absolutely destitute, standing outside the pale, suffering bitter moral anguish and loneliness.

By a stroke of supreme irony of fate Flora is rescued from death and isolation by a man who is *"a hermit* withdrawn from a wicked world," [17] a man who lives in solitude and silence. As a romantic outcast, Captain Anthony has a great deal in common with Lingard. If Conrad's women are passive, his men are generally very timid in their relationships with women. Even the villains, with a few exceptions (e.g., Ricardo in *Victory*), tend to exercise an unusual degree of courtesy toward their female victims. Conrad's own chivalry toward women is well-known. His romantic lovers are often chivalrous toward women to the point of absurdity. This, of course, derives mainly from the fact that his men, especially his seamen, are wholly unaccustomed to the company of girls of any kind. In the presence of women they are lost. Conrad's wife tells us that he

. . . had not the slightest notion how to take care of a young girl—a wife—not even from observation. What had he had of learning about married life? Not at school and still less on the high seas while his days ashore were intervals of utter loneliness. [28]

Marlow's attitude to the weaker sex reveals the similarity of his views with those of Conrad. He speaks more explicitly than Conrad himself:

For my part, in the presence of a young girl I always become convinced that *the dreams of sentiment*—like the consoling mysteries of Faith—are invincible, and *it is never, never* reason which governs men and women. [19]

Marlow tells us that Anthony had no experience whatever of women, and he could only have an ideal conception of his position. And since to Conrad an ideal is often but a flaming vision of reality, Anthony handled the delicate situation with utter simplicity, which was perhaps admirable but totally unsuitable for the occasion. Therefore, at the beginning he accomplished nothing by bringing Flora and her father aboard his ship. Marlow foresaw this when he doubted whether the circumstances of isolation at sea would alleviate the danger besetting poor Flora and Roderick. Ex-convict de Barral regards the ship as another prison, and Anthony not as his benefactor but as his jailer. Anthony is set apart from his crew, for the men under his command suspect that not all is well in the Captain's cabin, *"so unusually cut off from the rest of the ship . . ."* [20] His love for Flora is not like that of other men. It is a love born of a profound sense of pity. It is, in fact, something more than love,

. . . something as incredible as the fulfillment *of an amazing and startling dream* in which he could take the world in his arms—all the suffering world—not to possess its pathetic fairness but to console and cherish its sorrow. [21]

Anthony has an overwhelmingly strong capacity for tenderness of the fiery, predatory kind, "the tenderness of *silent, solitary men, the voluntary, passionate outcasts of their kind."* [22] Ironically, Marlow wonders whether one could have suspected him of being a heroic creature. The tone of his remarks indicates that he is angry with Anthony for being guilty of the kind of heroism which is idiotic, perhaps because it is the kind that takes the aspect of sublime delicacy. He is exasperated by the estrangement of Anthony and Flora on board the ship.

What could they have found to estrange them from each other with this rapidity and this thoroughness so far from all temptations, in the peace of the sea and *in an isolation so complete?* [23]

The son of the poet has inherited from his father his over-refined standard of delicacy. He has appropriated Flora de Barral but he does not know how to treat her. His action has been too sudden. Chance has thrown her in his way, and he must have indulged in fervent reveries to display such eagerness in his affection. Unfortunately, he cannot master his passion nor express it in words. This loss of self-control is the most dangerous thing to Conrad, who utters the following warning to the lover through Marlow's lips:

. . . *a passion, dominating or tyrannical, invading the whole man* and subjugating all his faculties to its own unique end, may conduct him whom it spurs and drives, into all sorts of adventures, to the brink of unfathomable dangers, to the limits of folly, and madness, and death.[24]

All Anthony had to do in order to end his and Flora's suffering was simply to tell her that he loved her. But his confounded delicacy made him afraid lest he offend her sensibilities. Flora, on the other hand, thought she was selling herself to him, and he was buying her out of sheer pity and secretly despised her. She discovers her love for Roderick Anthony through a tortuous process of rage and humiliation.

There is a similar situation in *Victory*. Lena and Heyst are isolated on a desolate island, yet they canont understand each other. Heyst's philosophy of complete detachment from the world has rendered him helpless in his relations with a woman. His heart is tender, but, like Anthony, he does not know what to say to Lena, or when to take her in his arms. Eventually, redemption is attained in *Chance* as well as in *Victory*. The Anthonys are luckier than Lena and Heyst in being able to live for a while after their mutual confession of love. Curiously enough, there must be at least one casualty in each case, as if Conrad wished to demonstrate that although the initial state of estrangement has been overcome, there can be no complete happiness. De Barral has to die so that Anthony and Flora might find each other's true love. Anthony must die so that Powell might win his Flora.

Although *Chance* is ostensibly a novel about middle-class English people, and its setting is far removed from that of *Almayer's Folly* and other "Malayan" stories, the men and women in it are as isolated as if they were cast out into the wilderness, where they lost the perception of reality. Even de Barral, the man of finance, and supposedly the man of the world, is a weak and confused man who understands neither the nature of his own business nor anything else. This great muddler of things is a selfish, petty man, doomed to perpetual loneliness despite his daughter's affection for him. When he emerges from prison, he regards the whole world as a hostile force and his daughter as his sole possession. Her marriage to Anthony he considers a betrayal of himself (Almayer also looks upon Nina's affection for Dain in a similar way). The world, his daughter and the "wicked captain" seem to be in league against him. This perfectly mediocre man completes the isolated trio on board the *Ferndale,* who are living an impossible existence of mental torment.

One can sense Marlow's impatience with the folly of these people, but his sympathy with the sufferers is greater than his irascibility. He shows considerable spiritual affinity with the isolatoes whose lives he investigates. His endless, melancholy (and at times somewhat cynical) comments on human nature make the reader suspect that he may also be suffering from some mystic wound which was inflicted upon his soul in the past. He is as forlorn as any of the participants in the tale which he unfolds. In fact, he readily lapses into a state of complete loneliness.

Arlette in *The Rover* is another persecuted damsel who also carries a psychic wound in her soul. The feelings she

inspires in the breast of Réal are akin to those experienced
by Anthony. Réal must undergo a veritable purgatory before his passion for Arlette is consummated. His love causes
in him mental anguish and extreme physical exhaustion,
a sensation experienced by all Conrad's lovers. He suffers
in loneliness until he is almost driven to suicide. Although
the story of these two lovers has a happy ending, it also has
a tragic touch. Peyrol, who takes Réal's place on a suicidal
mission, must be sacrificed on the altar of love and romantic
chivalry.

Geoffrey Renouard, whose passion for Felicia Moorsom
is as agonizing as that of Réal, is the victim of his own
weakness. Like Lingard, he is a successful man of action,
who controls the island Malata. But his security and strength
are instantly undermined by the appearance of the philosophy professor and his beautiful daughter. Felicia is seeking a man who once courted her and whom she had rejected. The man had worked for Renouard as an assistant
and died, but Renouard dares not reveal the truth to the
girl lest she depart from his island. Totally enslaved by
his sudden love for her, he creates for himself an imaginary world, in which Felicia is a dream-like, mysterious
creature, a sphinx. Felicia is nothing of the sort, of course,
but the romantic lover is blind to objective reality. He
cannot admit to himself that the object of his passion is not
willing or capable of returning his affection. Felicia is concerned only with her vanity, and she would rather devote
her life to the fictitious regard for the dead man than give
herself to the planter who wants her. As in *Victory* and
The Rescue, the man in love suffers intensely as though he
were in the grip of an overpowering disease.

Even an elemental type like Falk undergoes this purgatory when he falls in love, only to him consummation of
his desire is identical with satisfying his hunger. Falk,
who did not hesitate to eat a man in order to save his life,
wishes himself dead because he cannot win his girl. But

while Falk overcomes his moment of weakness and eventually triumphs, Renouard's will to live is destroyed by his failure to win Felicia. When she leaves the island he swims out into the open sea, his eyes fixed on a star. The loss of the adored woman is unbearable; it is fatal destiny itself.

We see thus that the theme of romantic love in Conrad cannot be divorced from the theme of isolation. Regardless of the outcome of a love-story, one or both of the lovers languish in painful, often deadly alienation from the human community, or else they are separated from each other by some insurmountable barrier. Sometimes the obstacle is the difference of race and cultural background (Lord Jim and Jewel, Willems and Aïssa). Sometimes there is a vast gap between the lovers' social status and their mental development, as in the case of Alice Jacobus and the Captain ("A Smile of Fortune"). Alice and her father are "a lonely pair of castaways on a desert island." [25] Jacobus lives in total isolation from the surrounding world, and his daughter knows nothing of life. She has been condemned "to *moral solitude* by the verdict of a respectable community." [26] The young Captain deludes himself that he is in love with this luckless illegitimate daughter of a pariah. He persists in seeing her despite her scornful attitude. Against his better judgment he makes a financial deal with her father, who sells him a load of seemingly useless potatoes. The seductiveness of Alice's scorn makes him feel "as if [my] innermost nature had been altered by the action of some *moral poison.*" [27] He experiences an abject dread of going to sea. His passion for Alice has made him forget his duty as a seaman. Yet he is doomed to be a stranger to her. She remains forever a mysterious and inscrutable being to him, and only when he has evoked a responsive affection in her heart does he realize clearly and with a sort of terror his "complete detachment from that unfortunate creature." [28] This cruel knowledge makes his feeling of guilt twofold, for he has now failed as a lover, too. The transaction with Jacobus has turned out a tremendous financial success owing to a scarcity of potatoes in the Captain's port of destination. When his firm wants to go on trading with Jacobus, the Captain decides to give up his command rather than risk another meeting with Alice. In a sense, this is also his atonement for having forgotten himself. At the end of the affair the disillusioned Captain reflects sadly that he

. . . had never felt *more isolated from the* rest of mankind than when [I] walked that day its crowded pavement, battling desperately with [my] thoughts and feeling already vanquished.[29]

If we accept Jean-Aubry's claim that "A Smile of Fortune" is autobiographical, we can safely assume that this is how Conrad himself must have felt when he discovered that a certain "Mademoiselle Eugénie" of Mauritius, with whom he had fallen in love and to whom he proposed, was already engaged. Conrad's resolution of the story is a fictional tit for tat directed at Mademoiselle Eugénie, in which not she but the Captain refuses to marry the girl.[30]

The rebuttal and the previous unhappy love affairs may have been responsible for the frequency with which Conrad's lovers are frustrated. His men are heart-broken or abandon themselves to their occupations while his women are silent and passive sufferers. Bessie Carvil, for example (in the story "To-Morrow"), cannot hope to win the heart of Harry Hagberd. He comes home after fifteen years of absence to find his father mad, with a fixed idea that his son would return "to-morrow." The old man does not recognize his son. Bessie Carvil, who has secretly been in love with the young sailor without having ever seen him, attempts to make him stay home. But it is useless, for the sailor prefers to keep his freedom. He leaves Bessie with her blind father and his own deranged father for a neighbor. He has destroyed her hopes and upset her quiet life.

Linda and Giselle in *Nostromo* are also left in despair
when Nostromo is shot by old Viola. Here, we have an additional obstacle—the tragic love conflict of the two sisters
who love the same man. Mrs. Gould, Nathalie Haldin,
Tekla, Mrs. Travers, Antonia, Amy Foster—in fact, almost
all Conrad's women are lonely and miserable. One wonders
whether this is so because of the "woman's belief that there
is nothing in the world but love—the everlasting thing." [31]
Are (all women, then, the victims of their hearts? A great
many, the student of Conrad will reply; but not all of
them. Besides, romantic love is not always the dominant
factor in women's lives. Winnie Verloc loves her brother
with motherly self-sacrifice. Mrs. Gould's affection for her
husband is also motherly, and Flora too divides her love
between her father and Anthony. But those women of Conrad, who believe in purity and duty and dignity, eventually
find out that they live in a world in which these virtues are
daily belied.

The fate of Conrad's isolatoes seems to follow a pattern
which occurs, with variations, throughout his work. The
protagonist is shown at the beginning as an innocent man,
a dreamer shut within his own illusory universe. A sudden
turn of fortune, usually an unexpected accident, creates a
dangerous moral situation, the solution of which may mean
life or death to the hero. But fate is not the only cause of
the misfortune which closes in upon the protagonist. The
real cause of disaster is, as often as not, within his own
ego. In Jim it is his romantic idealism, in Razumov his
cowardice and desire to be left alone, in Heyst his skepticism.

Lingard too senses that

. . . the real cause of disaster was somewhere else, was other,
and more remote. Lingard could not defend himself from a
feeling that it was in himself, too, somewhere in *the unexplored
depths of his nature, something fatal and unavoidable.*[32]

As no hero of Conrad can escape from himself, Lingard's steering north in order to get away from the yacht (which is heading south) with Mrs. Travers, is as ineffective as Jim's flight to Patusan or Razumov's attempt to escape responsibility for his betrayal. These men are doomed to loneliness in the first place because, being different from other people, they respond sensitively to the "shadowy appeals" of their imagination. Each must remain imprisoned within his romantic ago.

Jim's problem is more complex than anything Almayer or Lingard have experienced. It is at first hard to see what is wrong with this gentlemanly and tractable young man who has a thorough knowledge of his duties and outwardly displays no peculiarities save for physical toughness and a look of resoluteness. He is clean-limbed and clean faced— the kind of fellow one would leave in charge of a ship on the strength of his looks.

However, Jim's sound looks are shockingly deceptive, and the truth of the matter is simply that it would *not* have been safe to trust the deck to him. Marlow is horrified by this contrast between the young man's appearance and his performance in the moment of danger. The trouble with Jim, Marlow patiently explains, is the man's swift and forestalling imagination which, in Conrad's opinion is "the enemy of men, the father of all terrors." [33] It is imagination, among other reasons, that separates Jim from the rest of mankind and makes him live in the dream world of romantic achievement, which is as real to him as the windmills were to Don Quixote.

Jim does not regard the ship as a place where men earn their living, but rather as a carrier into the lands of his dreams, which will provide him with an opportunity to show his many-sided courage. He and the other four men live amidships in isolation from the human cargo, but Jim has nothing in common with these men. He is separated from them by a gulf that cannot be crossed. The sea means to him (as it does to Marlow) glamor and romance. The dreams, more real than the actual monotony of an uneventful passage, breed in him an exaggerated self-confidence. All men could flinch in a moment of danger, but he felt sure—he alone would know how to deal with the spurious menace of wind and seas. Perhaps he could have become the hero he wished to be had he not taken the post of the chief mate of a ship without ever having been tested by the events of the sea that reveal man's inner worth to others and to himself. This lack of experience coupled with Jim's exuberant imagination constitutes the crux of his dilemma. The disparity between his idealized vision of himself and his humiliating defeat in reality is intolerable.

The isolating and destructive influence of his imagination shows first when he fails to respond quickly in an emergency. Instead of rushing to the rescue of a man who has fallen overboard, Jim watches the accident as if confounded. Only a little while ago he saw himself saving people from disaster. In this vision he appeared as a solitary castaway, struggling for survival. He fought savages on tropical shores, quelled mutinies on the high seas; he cheered up his men when they were cast adrift in a small boat, always setting an example of devotion to duty. Now was his chance to show his unflinching heroism—and he lost it. He was too late. He did *not* jump overboard to save the drowning man. The first opportunity was gone and he experienced the pain of defeat.

It was himself that he saw in all those exploits. What appealed to him was applause, a desire for admiration as a hero, and not the actual saving of people or performing the arduous task of steering a ship to safety. Conrad defines this egotism as a sort of sublimated, idealized selfishness. Jim's egocentric feeling reached such a degree that when the real crisis came and he failed again, it assumed tragic proportions. The precious world of his dreams was blown to bits the moment he leaped from the *Patna*. From now on he was "a solitary man confronted by his fate."[34]

Jim does not understand his own motives for the desertion, or perhaps is unable to admit to himself the true reason for his second failure: a moment of cowardice. The tragic aspect of the case is enhanced by Jim's stubborn quest for self-discovery, which is the true conflict of the book. He must explain to himself *why* he has jumped, and when the true meaning of the act dawns upon him he realizes that there is no going back for him.

Deprived of his license, Jim is an outcast, a sailor in exile from the sea. He yearns for rehabilitation, but, like Almayer, he cannot forget. The memory of the ghastly night torments him. And worse than the memory is the thought that he has missed a great chance in his life. His exalted vanity cannot bear the idea. He will seek for a way to come back among people as a trusted and honorable man. He will also receive punishment for the heroics of his fancy; he must expiate the transgression of desiring more glamor than he could carry. He is as isolated in his grief and remorse as he was in his dreams of future achievements. In the remote corner of the world where he attempts to regain his honor,

... *he was protected by his isolation, alone of his own superior kind*, in close touch with Nature, that keeps faith on such easy terms with her lovers.[35]

The force of imagination which creates another reality for him, superior to that of physical reality, has deprived him of the moral contact with other people. Overwhelmed by the inexplicable, he is baffled by his own personality. But he never gives up his dreams, nor does he let the *Patna* incident lapse into oblivion. The isolation of the romantic dreamer was to him a pleasant burden, if it was a burden at all. But the moral isolation that follows his desertion of the *Patna* is extremely hard to endure. He feels cut off from the rest of his kind, like a trapped beast, trying to escape from an enclosure of high stakes.

The conflict within Jim reaches a paradoxical point. In order to retrieve his honor Jim must lose it in the court. In order to come back to the world he must get away from it. But the latter would mean again a total renunciation of his major dream—to win the recognition of the world. Retiring into loneliness Jim cannot even be certain he will attain redemption in his own eyes. A similar antinomy results when Jim attempts to explain to others what is inscrutable to himself.

It is a vicious circle. Jim's dispute is with an invisible personality, "an antagonistic and inseparable partner of his existence—another possessor of his soul." [36] Unwilling to admit that he has been betrayed by his own nature, he believes that some mysterious impulse must have driven him to that abject leap from the *Patna*. In both failures Jim was incapable of action because of his "isolating imagination" which made him *watch* the incidents rather than act. He had been taken unawares, thrown into a crisis from a state of the most perfect security which was given to him by his vanity. Jim's moment of cowardice has revealed his own nature to him. From now on, he is haunted by a sense of defeat. It is a kind of egoism which can be assuaged only by death or an act of supreme self-sacrifice.

Does this mean that one *cannot* run away from the world, that it will always overtake us and wreak vengeance for our loneliness? Does it mean that one *ought not* to "leave the ranks" for the catastrophe is then bound to happen, and, moreover, it is just? Both of these are implied, and it is the latter that enhances Jim's tragic aspect, for what else has been left him but an escape from the world?

This escape, Jim believes, will help him not only to rehabilitate himself but also to find an answer to the tormenting question: "Why did he jump that fateful night?" His quest for self-knowledge is paralleled, if not exceeded, by Marlow's own quest and by his "probing" attitude toward the young man. Why, it can be asked, is Marlow so preoccupied with the fortunes of Jim? Why is Brierly? The reason is the same as the reasons for Jim's romantic behavior: the search for truth. Marlow is fascinated by the mystery of Jim's attitude, and the obscure truth involved in his case appears to him momentous enough to influence mankind's conception of itself. This truth, Marlow points out, may be revealed in a moment of illusion and in a state of extreme solitude.

I only know that I stood there long enough for the *sense of utter solitude* to get hold of me so completely that all I had lately seen, all I had heard, and the very human speech itself, seemed to have passed out of existence.[37]

In trying to probe the unfathomable, Marlow resembles Jim who endeavors to achieve his goal although in his heart of hearts he senses ultimate failure. Marlow seeks for clues to his own personality in Jim's life.

There is in Jim's fate a sort of profound and *terrifying logic* as if it were our *imagination alone* that could set loose upon us the might of an *overwhelming destiny*.[38]

The logic is terrifying to Marlow and to Brierly because Jim's story appears to them as an illuminating symbol shedding light upon their own lives. Because they are endowed with the same vivid imagination that Jim possesses, they become involved in his life. For they, too, fear to get trapped by destiny, whose incalculable decrees plunge men into the pit of isolation. Time and again destiny descends swiftly and finally upon the characters of Conrad. Almayer, Lingard, Kurtz, Heyst, Kayerts, Carlier, Razumov, Decoud, Nostromo . . . one could go on enumerating almost all of his protagonists.

Paradoxically, some souls can achieve greatness only if

isolated. Jim's sacrifice can be regarded by some, as it was by the recipient of Marlow's letter, as pointless unless he believed in its necessity and its justice. Without that belief the sacrifice is a mere search for forgetfulness. Marlow's friend advocates the view that the sacrifice of the white man's life is justified if it is made in the name of ideas which promote the white man's order and morality. Jim's giving up his life to "them," meaning to all of mankind with skins brown, yellow or black in color was like selling his soul to a brute.

Marlow disagrees with this racial theory. The point, he maintains,

. . . is that of all mankind *Jim had dealings but with himself* (like Lingard) and the question is whether at the last he had not confessed to a faith mightier than the laws of order and progress.[39]

Jim is very different from Kipling's heroes. Kipling's protagonists, often isolated in a foreign culture, are invariably the carriers of "the white man's burden." They are not distinguished by, or shall we say plagued with, the sort of romantic imagination that destroys Lord Jim, Lingard, Renouard and other characters of Conrad. Moreover, Kipling, unlike Conrad, is not interested in the psychological probing into man's nature. A few strokes, often masterful indeed, are sufficient to portray a man. Kipling is not engaged in a search for motives. To Conrad, on the other hand, this search is the essence of his art. Kipling simplifies the human soul. Conrad finds emotional and philosophical complexity even in most simple-minded creatures.

Take Nostromo, for example. In the beginning, he is an extrovert, not given to introspection. But in the course of the novel Nostromo turns into a man tortured by remorse and doubt. A man whose life rests on his reputation, he would die rather than sully his perfect egoism. In comparison with Nostromo Jim is a strong man, for he never gives up his romantic dream. Nostromo is concerned solely with the gratification of his boundless vanity. His incorruptibility is only a veneer plastered on a fundamental moral irresponsibility. But Jim lives up to the maxim of his father, who taught him that he who once yields to temptation hazards total depravity and everlasting ruin. Therefore, man should never do anything he believes to be wrong. Jim prepared to fling away his daily bread in order to grapple with a ghost, because the question for him was not how to get rid of his affliction but how to live.

Conrad, the romantic, cannot be divorced from the traditions of Polish romanticism. It is very hard, however, to trace a direct "influence" of Polish romantic poetry, or of Polish literature of later periods, on Conrad's work. Conrad persistently refrained from writing on Poland and her problems, but there is a certain spiritual and moral "atmosphere" in his work, which brings him close to some Polish masters of literature, particularly when he deals with the problem of the individual and his relation to society and also in his treatment of love.

In his recent book, *Joseph Conrad: Achievement and Decline*,[40] Thomas Moser speaks of Conrad's attitude toward love and sex, pointing out the shift in Conrad's themes, from explorations into moral failure in the masculine world (that had enabled him to achieve artistic success) to the frustrating subject of love. Conrad's negative attitude toward love should not be shocking or surprising, Mr. Moser asserts, since Conrad sees man as lonely and morally isolated, troubled by egoistic longing for power and peace, stumbling along a perilous past, his only hope benumbing labor or, in rare cases, a little self-knowledge. Conrad could not possibly reconcile so gloomy a view with a belief in the panacea of love, wife, home, and family. Thus, the effect of sexual subject matter on Conrad's creative processes was inhibiting and crippling.

Mr. Moser claims that when Lingard tells Willems that he is not a man at all, he refers to Willems's sexual potency. This does not seem plausible. The Lingard of *An Outcast of the Islands* is not the Lingard of *The Rescue*. In the former novel Lingard is furious with Willems *only* because of his betrayal. Willems is not a man to Lingard because he lacks those attributes of faithfulness which Lingard takes for granted; because he has no loyalty.

That Aïssa's appeal to Willems is sexual is quite obvious. But it must be borne in mind that Willems falls under the spell of her physical charm *after* his initial moral corruption. Mr. Moser contends that in *An Outcast of the Islands* the life of the forest producing death is equated with woman; perhaps it is. Aïssa is a symbolic character, but it is not love that destroys Willems and therefore the main thesis of Mr. Moser lacks cogency. Willems's passion for the savage Aïssa is brief not because Willems has exhausted his sexual potency (as Mr. Moser would have us believe), but because he has failed in his attempt to escape from his guilt. The seeds of his self-destruction are mentioned on the first page of the novel, where his failure to conceive the moral significance of his acts is described. Carol Reed's film version of the book is eminently successful in showing the sensual aspect of Willems's passion, particularly by way of such devices as the "Marathon kiss." Yet the novel's central theme is *not* sensual love and its consequences but rather the inner conflict in Willems— his moral deterioration which begins *before* he meets Aïssa. The latter can be regarded as a symbol of the retribution meted out by the fates to Willems for his treachery, and not the primary cause of his tragedy. She is merely the instrument of destiny.

Mr. Moser correctly emphasizes Conrad's use of jungle imagery, but the images of trees, creepers, flowers, fertility and decay are employed not solely for the purpose of conveying Conrad's subterranean emotions concerning love **but** mainly to express the full meaning of man's inescapable loneliness and his moral dilemma. Mr. Moser interprets the description of the forests, fertility and death in *Almayer's Folly* as Conrad's subconscious desire to underline the femininity of the destructive jungle life. The consummation of love between Dain and Nina is associated with death. Yet Mr. Moser himself notices a symbolic use of similar imagery in "Youth," where the mysterious East appears to Marlow, "silent like death, dark like a grave." Here Mr. Moser makes no attempt to locate significant sexual symbolism.

Perhaps it is true that Conrad fails in his presentation of sexual love between man and woman, but this does not mean an artistic failure of the novelist. I suppose it is possible to dissect Conrad's fiction in a thoroughly clinical manner and show that some of his "immobilized" lovers are either impotent or voyeuristic. Whether this kind of approach will shed more light on the more subtle meanings of Conrad's fiction is debatable. Yet the implication, albeit made with certain reservations, of Conrad's own sexual impotence will surely be questioned by many critics (and readers) who have always regarded Conrad as a "masculine" writer.

To do justice to Mr. Moser's thesis, one must not wax sentimental over any unpleasant discoveries about Conrad, the man and the writer. The problem remains and it has to be explained. Why did Conrad fail in his description of sexual intimacy? I should like to suggest that love as such is not an uncongenial subject with Conrad, but that his treatment of sex reveals Conrad's vision of mankind. Man dreams of honor and glory but he is usually left with a sense of profound loneliness when he comes to understand the true disparity between dream and reality. Sexual love promises the closest union between man and woman but, in Conrad's fiction, it usually brings solitude. Perhaps this is Conrad's way of dramatizing the human condition— as he sees it. In his view of humanity people are separated by great distances that cannot be bridged by sexual contact. Conrad's luckless and frustrated lovers are not different from his luckless and frustrated dreamers who seek romantic adventure and pursue honor. Their inability to love is actually their inability to come close to one another; it is their expression of irremediable individualism. This is consistent with Conrad's professed view of life:

Everybody must walk in the light of his own gospel. . . . No man's light is good to any of his fellows. That's my view of life—a view that rejects all formulas, dogmas and principles of other people's making. These are a web of illusions. We are too varied. Another's man's truth is only a dismal lie to me.[41]

It would be difficult to reconcile this extreme belief in individualism with the idea of a romantic merging of two bodies and souls. I suspect that one reason why Conrad strikes the critic as "modern" is precisely his treatment of love relationship, in which man does not shed his basic isolation. But when people cannot love they are even more isolated. Conrad's lovers, like his traitors, repeatedly express Razumov's sentiment: "I am independent—and therefore perdition is my lot." [42]

I find it hard to accept the psychoanalytical interpretation that love is the key to the understanding of Conrad's works. The spectacle of "menacing female sexuality" which Mr. Moser finds almost everywhere, and the persistent implication that Conrad and his heroes are sexually impotent, cannot give a full explanation of Conrad's protagonists. Sex alone does not account for the passivity of his women nor for the diffidence of his men. Polish and European romantic writers, Conrad's experiences as a sailor, and, above all, the tradition of patriarchal Polish landed gentry from which Conrad came—these are some of the *other* factors that undoubtedly influenced his treatment of love.

Mr. Moser suggests that Almayer's love for Nina is in-

cestuous, and so is de Barral's for Flora and Ortega's for
Rita (in *The Sisters*). Perhaps Mr. Moser expects Conrad
to see the relationship between parents and children from
the point of view of a modern American; perhaps he
exaggerates the role of sex in the lives of Conrad's protagonists. Whatever the case, he fails to take notice of Conrad's early upbringing. In the Poland of Conrad's youth
parents tended to be rather autocratic and the relationship
of father to daughter was usually patriarchal. Almayer's
love for Nina is great and therefore it must be "possessive"
but it is also self-sacrificing. And de Barral's egoistic love
for Flora is not necessarily incestuous. He is a selfish man,
and his motives in plotting against Anthony are not those
of a frustrated lover. It is also known that Conrad himself
was not a patient and tolerant parent. His son John recalls
him as a very furious man, and his son Borys incurred
Conrad's violent wrath for daring to marry without his
consent. It seems to me, therefore, that Conrad's attitude
toward women and love comes partly from what he himself
accepted as the romantic chivalrous tradition of the Polish
landed gentry in the Ukraine, and from the tradition of
Polish romantic poetry.

Conrad's treatment of love often resembles that of the
Polish romantic poets. Let us examine a few examples from
the "big three" of Polish romantic poetry: Adam Mickiewicz
(1798–1855), Juliusz Slowacki (1809–1849), and Zygmunt
Krasinski (1812–1859). *Dziady* (Forefathers's Eve) is by
Mickiewicz, whose work Conrad knew very well and from
whose poems he occasionally transcribed whole passages. A
few poignant illustrations of this influence by Mickiewicz
were pointed out by Professor Ludwik Krzyzanowski in
his article about "Prince Roman." [43] Although there seem to
be no direct stylistic references in Conrad's novels and
tales to the text of *Dziady*, the latter poetic work contains
several leitmotivs which one easily finds in Conrad.

Gustaw, the hero of *Dziady*, commits suicide because of

a disappointment in love. He is reincarnated as Konrad (after whom Joseph Conrad was named) who symbolizes man's destiny. The suicide itself is also symbolic, and the woman merely an agent of man's fate. The inner moral transformation is the key to this and to almost all other important works of Mickiewicz. Konrad is an idealized Promethean Patriot who cries out against God for allowing mankind *and* Poland to suffer. What makes Konrad a true hero is a love which is infinitely more than an infatuation with a woman; Konrad loves his country more passionately than another man loves his mistress. For Mickiewicz, declares a famous modern Polish poet, "the manifestations of the heroic spirit precede the crystallization of love, and . . . he conceived of heroism as a primordial instinct as the instinct of love." [44]

Love of woman for the Polish romantic poets is often not far removed from their dreams of hero leadership and the sense of mission. Possessed by the ideal of saving their people (mostly without the people themselves) the Polish romantic heroes trust only their own effort and heroism, ever ready to give their lives in the service of Poland. And, like Conradian heroes, they wage a constant battle against pitiless destiny. Sometimes their cause is victorious despite their sacrifice, as in the case of Mickiewicz's Konrad Wallenrod and Krasinski's Iridion (in the drama *Iridion).* Sometimes it is doomed to perdition, e.g., in the tragedy of the Weneds and their inevitable destruction (in Slowacki's tragedy *Lilla Weneda),* and in the posthumous victories of Anhelli (in Slowacki's drama *Anhelli)* and Iridion.

Through the figure of Anhelli, Slowacki expresses his unshakable belief in the value of disinterested suffering and the necessity for self-sacrifice. Anhelli must die in loneliness in the icy wastes of the north, but his death is not purposeless, for it is followed by the appearance of a symbolic knight who heralds the beginning of a universal revolution. The capacity for boundless self-sacrifice is one of the most distinctive characteristics of the Polish romantic hero in literature and in life. These heroes are Titanic figures who hold themselves responsible for the fate of their country, and who, after a period of intense suffering and self-immolation, perish for the sake of their ideals. Consider two protagonists of Mickiewicz: Grazyna and Konrad Wallenrod, and the affinity of the Conradian romantic characters with them becomes quite obvious. Both characters embrace betrayal—in order to further what they consider the true cause of fidelity. They will deny themselves the consolations of vanity and, despite occasional waverings, will pursue their course steadfastly to the inevitable, tragic death.

Grazyna, A Tale of Lithuania is a short romantic epic which narrates the struggle of the Lithuanians in the fourteenth century against the German Knights of the Cross. The heroine is the wife of the Lithuanian prince, Litawor, who plots with the German knights against his Lithuanian foe, prince Witold. Defending her land and her husband's good name, Grazyna dons his armor and leads the Lithuanians against the Knights of the Cross. She is mortally wounded and before she dies she pleads with Litawor to forgive her "first and last unfaithfulness." Litawor weeps; and when his wife is placed on the sacrificial funeral pyre he leaps into the flames.

Konrad Wallenrod is a romantic tale in the Byronic tradition. It describes the tragic life of a fourteenth-century Lithuanian, kidnapped in childhood by the Knights of the Cross. Konrad Wallenrod's life in captivity is sustained by his determination to wreak terrible vengeance upon the enemies of his country. When he becomes Grand Master of the Order he purposely mismanages a campaign against the Lithuanians, causing the defeat of the Knights of the Cross. But although the moral of both *Grazyna* and *Konrad Wallenrod* is that deceit and treachery are honorable if employed for patriotic purposes, these acts end in tragic death. Konrad Wallenrod's dream of revenge has come true;

but in attaining victory over his foes he has suffered a personal moral defeat. His moral dilemma lies in the recognition of his own duplicity as morally evil. He wants no more bloodshed, no more treason or vengeance. "Germans, too, are men," he declares before his act of self-sacrifice which brings him final release from his inner torment.

These heroes of Mickiewicz are great moral sufferers. The Konrad of *The Forefathers' Eve, Part III* is no different in this respect. He is a selfless poet whose name, he believes to be Million, because he loves millions and he suffers for millions. And the humble monk Robak (or Jacek Soplica) of the great poetic epic, *Pan Tadeusz*, belongs to the same moral type of man. Having killed his foe in a moment of wrath, this grand, romantic soul spends the rest of his days in the service of his nation and family until the moment of his supreme sacrifice.

The heroes of Slowacki share this faculty of self-sacrifice with both Mickiewicz's and Krasinski's characters. In a press interview with Marian Dabrowski in 1914 Conrad spoke thus about his indebtedness to Poland:

—Immortality of Poland? You—we. Who doubts it? The English critics—after all, I am indeed an English writer—speaking of me, always add that there is in me something incomprehensible, unfathomable, impalpable. You alone can understand the incomprehensible, conceive the impalpable. *It is Polishness.* The Polishness which I took into my works through Mickiewicz and Slowacki. My father read *Pan Tadeusz* aloud to me and made me read it out loud. Not once, not twice. I preferred *Konrad Wallenrod, Grazyna.* Later I preferred Slowacki. Do you know why Slowacki? *Il est l'âme de toute la Pologne, lui.*[45]

One of the most interesting characters of Slowacki is Kordian who is the protagonist of a poetic drama of this name. Like Anhelli, Kordian dreams of saving his country, and gives his life for it. And, like Lord Jim, he suffers from his own imagination. It is the excessive sensibility of his nature that paralyzes him with fear at the time of the first test (or shall we say trial?) of his moral mettle, when he is about to kill the Tsar. A simple man of action, entrusted with the task of assassination may occasionally lose heart and flee from danger. But it is only the highly imaginative man who will remain on the scene, rooted to the spot, unable to act in the most crucial moment of his life. Thus it is with Kordian, with Jim, with Lingard of *The Rescue*. Kordian's discourse with the Doctor, in the hospital for the insane, serves the same purpose that Jim's long talks with Marlow do—it sheds light on the reasons of the hero's weakness and his later "redemption" by means of self-sacrifice. Says Kordian to the Doctor:

> Every man who sacrifices himself
> For freedom's sake—is a man, a new creation of God.[46]

The Doctor questions the validity of Kordian's sacrifice, and in a moment of despair Kordian exclaims:

> . . . Oh, Satan!
> You have come here to kill the soul of my soul:
> You're taking my last treasure, *my own conviction:*
> And you extinguish the last ray.[47]

Yet Kordian dies proudly, facing the execution squad of the Tsar (as Jim faces Doramin's pistol), unaware that the Grand Duke is speeding with the Tsar's pardon. Kordian's vision of himself as the savior of his nation has not come true, as Jim's vision of himself as the splendid romantic hero of the seas has not been fulfilled. The romantic ideal has set these two men apart from their fellow-men and it has led to ruin rather than to glory. Unless, of course, one considers their failure to be in the nature of a moral victory. If one does so, one immediately perceives the difference between the two characters. Slowacki's hero dies in an attempt to save his nation, and he has no choice in the matter. Jim *can* escape death, but he sacrifices himself in atonement for the death of Dain, which can hardly be considered a true redemption for it merely soothes his injured vanity. One can never be certain whether this kind of a "redemption" has not been colored with a tinge of irony. Kordian is not quite devoid of vanity, either; in his last hours he seeks the spurious immortality of having his name borne by the old servant's grandson. He is resigned, almost in a philosophically detached mood. But standing before the execution squad he attains true glory, for he is finally identified with the people, and the Grand Duke is desperately trying to save his life. His crime of conspiracy against the Tsar or his failure to kill him (depending on one's point of view), his solitary stand on behalf of his country—these transgressions are punished in the same manner in the drama of Slowacki and the novel of Conrad. In Krasinski's drama *Iridion* the hero is possed by the idea of vengeance (not unlike Konrad Wallenrod and Grazyna) which develops into a great patriotic mission. Again, the hero is not interested in his own glory but is dedicated to the higher duty of serving his brethren. And, finally, Count Henry of Krasinski's *Nieboska Komedia* (The Undivine Comedy) is another man who must undergo a profound moral conflict in his attempt to defend the bastion of the now degenerated aristocracy against the onslaught of democracy.

Conrad knew well this spirit of Polish romantic poetry. It is not unnatural, therefore, that his only distinctly Polish story, "Prince Roman," has a hero in the tradition of Polish romanticism. The influence of Polish patriotism can be found also in the thematically non-Polish novel *Nostromo*. In the "Author's Note" Conrad explains his attachment to the beautiful Antonia:

. . . why not be frank about it?— . . . the true reason is that I have modelled her on my first love. How we . . . used to look up to that girl just out of the schoolroom herself, as the *standard-bearer* of a faith to which we were all born, but which she alone knew how to hold aloft with an unflinching hope! She had perhaps more glow and less serenity in her soul than Antonia, but she was *an uncompromising Puritan of patriotism, with no taint of the slightest worldliness in her thoughts.*[48]

What appealed to Conrad so profoundly was not merely the fact of Antonia's "model" being his first love, but the power of her conviction and her Puritan self-denial. Thus it is that Prince Roman's words "from conviction" assume dramatic significance. Antonia is not the only person in *Nostromo* to hold firm beliefs. Nostromo's is a *"faithful devotion* with something despairing as well as desperate in its impulses." [49] The man's predicament is clearly indicated in the following description:

. . . the trusted, the wealthy comrade Fidanza with the knowledge of his *mortal ruin* locked up in his breast, he remains essentially a Man of the People. In his mingled love and scorn of life and *in the bewildered conviction of having been betrayed* he hardly knows by what or by whom, he is still of the People, their undoubted Great Man—with a private history of his own.[50]

Admittedly, Nostromo's betrayal and redemption are treated with an irony that is rarely found in the typical Polish romantic poets, but the preoccupation with fidelity is there, and it is this preoccupation of Conrad that is basically responsible for his turning novelist—if we are to believe his own words. For this is how he describes the appeal Almayer held for him:

What made you [Almayer] so real to me was that you held this lofty theory with *some force of conviction* and with an admirable consistency.[51]

This is exactly the fascination of Jim for Marlow who tells us that,

The whisper of *his conviction* seemed to open before me a vast and uncertain expanse. . . . His life had begun in sacrifice, in enthusiasm for generous ideas . . . no one could be more romantic than himself.[52]

Men like Jim and Nostromo are conceived in the tradition of Polish romanticism, but only in a limited sense. The heroes of Mickiewicz, Slowacki and Krasinski are torn by an inner conflict; they are, however, defeated by the forces of destiny more than by their own imperfections. Their dreams are more grandiose than the dreams of Conrad's romantic figures who often are a far cry from the Polish, Titanic heroes. Moreover, the frequently ironic tone of Conrad's commentators robs his heroes of the genuine heroic character they may possess. No one doubts the heroic quality of Iridion or Konrad Wallenrod; but Jim, Nostromo and Marlow are cut of a different mettle.

Their romantic dreams reveal the fundamental discrepancy between illusion and reality. An older dreamer, like Stein, recognizes the appalling incongruity of life—that man's dreams may not be attained, and yet he must forever dream. Stein is also a realist in being able to understand the true nature of romantic dreams. He knows that reality must close down inexorably upon man, and the dream may turn into a destructive nightmare; but the realist gives in to the romantic.

What makes a romantic dream lose its appeal and change into a nightmare is primarily its paralyzing power. Lord Jim and the Lingard of *The Rescue* are unable to act in the most crucial moments of their lives. Although Lingard does not experience Jim's inability to act as a result of psychic identification with another person (since neither Mrs. Travers nor her husband can take Brown's place), his nature is as romantic as Jim's. In his acts

. . . performed simply, *from conviction,* what may be called the romantic side of the man's nature came out; *that responsive sensitiveness to the shadowy appeals* made by life and death which is the groundwork of a *chivalrous character*.[53]

The romantic appears also in the Polish novel of the nineteenth and twentieth centuries. Conrad knew the work of such writers as Boleslaw Prus (1847–1912) and Stefan Zeromski (1864–1925), to mention two masters of the Polish prose with whom he shows some affinity. Wokulski, the hero of Prus's *Lalka* (Doll), who impresses everybody with his realism, is a romantic at heart. He has risen from poverty to wealth and social prominence, but his hopeless love for a frigid and spoiled young woman from the aristocratic circles brings him to ruin and self-destruction. Wokulski's infatuation with Isabella Lecka (the "doll") proves as disastrous as Lingard's passion for Mrs. Travers. Each creates an image of his beloved which does not correspond to reality. Each betrays the trust that other people put in him. Wokulski cannot escape from his dream of Isabella although, like Lingard and Renouard, he has finally seen her true face. That other image, the idealized one, will pursue him forever. In order to escape from it he must disappear from this world. There is another great dreamer in the novel, somewhat recalling Marlow—"the last romantic," Rzecki, who is immersed in his Napoleonic illusion to the last, and is as painstaking an observer of his beloved boss Wokulski, as Marlow is of his protégé, Jim.

Conrad has a great deal in common with Zeromski, whom he met in Poland in 1904 and with whom he later corresponded. Zeromski wrote a preface to a Polish translation of Conrad's work and a critical article about him. His masterpiece, *Ludzie bezdomni* (The Homeless Man), was written in the same year as *Lord Jim* (1900). Its main protagonist, Dr. Judym, is as egotistic in his devotion to social ideals as Jim is to his concept of heroism and personal honor. Jim can have no personal happiness until he has paid the debt he owes to his own conscience. Dr. Judym, the self-educated cobbler's son, can have neither father nor mother nor wife. He has devoted himself to the cause of bettering the lot of the poor in order to pay his "accursed debt," and, like Jim, he rejects the woman who loves him. Each man pursues his dream unflinchingly, refusing, in Stein's words, to keep still on his heap of mud.

Conrad's dreamers surround themselves with the shadows of their imagination, which bewilder them because they resemble the realities of life. They challenge their destiny, ignoring their chance for a smug and comfortable life—when they have such a chance. The realization that their struggle may be futile will not deter them from submitting to Stein's exalted romantic credo: "To follow the dream, and again to follow the dream—and so always—*usque ad finem . . .*" [54]

CHAPTER **III**

THE BALANCE OF
COLOSSAL FORCES[1]

To CONRAD, AS TO HARDY, nature is a senseless mechanical power. He regards life as a spectacle in which the forces of nature sometimes play a symbolical part. Both the impenetrable, somber forests and the vast solitude of waters, to use Conrad's familiar epithets, become in his books factors that shape human destiny. This vision of nature is essentially romantic, although the protagonists affected by it are not necessarily romantic characters (as in the sad story "An Outpost of Progress"). The Romantic finds himself in nature. The mountains, the rivers, the sea, the moon and the sun are to him symbols of his own personality. The struggle against the elements shows man's inner worth not only to others but also to himself. It is a test which ultimately brings self-knowledge.

Cut off from land, the men aboard ship are exposed to entirely new dangers and living conditions, and hence are governed by different concepts of morals and justice. The crew, as a social group, lives in isolation, but its captain's solitude may be said to be twofold. He shares his men's lot, but at the same time he must bear the responsibility of command—a powerfully "separating" agent.

The task of a ship's crew is keeping the vessel afloat and following a given course. It can be performed only if the work is executed by a compact body of sailors obeying the commands of their superiors. But the fury of the elements may destroy their valuable solidarity.

This is the disintegrating power of a great wind: *it isolates one from one's kind.* An earthquake, a landslip, an avalanche, overtake a man incidentally, as it were—without a passion. A furious gale attacks him like a personal enemy, tries to grasp his limbs, fastens upon his mind, seeks to rout his very spirit out of him.[2]

What the crew faces is not a problem of the sea but merely

. . . a problem that has arisen on board a ship where *the conditions of complete isolation from all land entanglements* make it stand out with a particular force and coloring.[3]

These conditions make the dying Negro sailor of the *Narcissus* the center of the ship's collective psychology. A Negro in the British forecastle, Conrad observes, is a lonely being, for he has no friends. But despite his separateness imposed on him by his color, James Wait is able to exercise an uncanny influence on the entire crew because he has changed from a mere sickly sailor into a symbol of Fate itself. His stubborn, though inert struggle with death is paralleled by the crew's clash with the brute forces of the elements. Out of their fight for self-preservation a solidarity is born which can defeat, or at least subdue to some extent, the sense of isolation reigning on board the *Narcissus*. Without this sense of fellowship the crew is reduced to a state of anarchy which makes the isolation of the ship unbearable. The captain's firmness restores the identity and the unity of the crew at a moment when fear has turned them into unthinking animals. Yet they remain, in a sense, apart from the rest of humanity, even when united among themselves. They appear to be

. . . creatures of another kind—lost, alone, forgetful and doomed;
they were like castaways, like reckless and joyous castaways,
like mad castaways. . . .*[4]

In the story "Falk" Conrad shows what happens to a
crew of a ship isolated in the open sea and possessed by
the spectre of starvation. Here we have no raging storms to
assail the sailors and thus draw them together under the
command of the captain. The solidarity of the men aboard
disintegrates. Each man is alone and only the fittest will
survive. The safe and comfortable ship has become a floating coffin, and the men in it savages.

The Falks, Singletons, MacWhirrs, Beards and Allistouns are not romantic dreamers. Their sole preoccupation
being good service and survival in a struggle with the sea,
they can find no driving impulse within themselves toward
the path of adventure. Lacking imagination, they have no
dream or illusion of their own which might set them apart
from their fellows. If they too are isolated, like their romantic comrades of the sea, Lord Jim, Marlow, Lingard and
Anthony, the cause of their predicament is different. Not
their imagination, but the nature of their task is the isolating factor. During a gale the crew of Captain MacWhirr
were cheered up by the mere presence of their chief on
deck, but he himself

. . . could expect no relief of that sort from any one on earth.
Such is the *loneliness of command.*[5]

The "strong magic of command" separates the captain from
his crew. Often, the responsibility for the lives of men and
for the safety of the ship and its cargo evokes in the captain a feeling of self-mistrust. This is how young Conrad

felt when he first assumed command of a ship.[6] And this is also, on a different plane, how Conrad the writer felt when he embarked on his quest as an artist. The captain's sense of "catastrophic loneliness" changed to *"conditions of moral isolation"* under which he worked.[7]

Needless to say, self-mistrust of the person in charge not only causes him to shun his fellows lest they should learn of his doubts and fears, but also breeds remorse in his mind when something goes wrong. Although the atmosphere of the supernatural, savoring of "The Ancient Mariner," is not often evoked in the works of Conrad, the "sickness of the soul" which is the result of remorse, is a familiar theme. The young Captain in *The Shadow Line,* who had to bear the strain of Burns' moral shock and his superstitious fancy, admits that no confessed criminal had ever been so crushed by his sense of guilt. The Captain in "The Secret Sharer" also suffers from a sense of troubled incertitude. Going through the process of trial and self-knowledge, he discovers that he is a stranger to the crew and to himself.

"The Secret Sharer" and *The Shadow Line* are symbolic studies of man's self-awareness, particularly of his subconscious mind. As the Captain in "The Secret Sharer" wears a sleeping-suit (a symbol of the subconscious) so does the skipper in *The Shadow Line* throughout the period of trouble. The young commanders must find out that the meeting between man and his darker self is dangerous. They can combat the foe of self-distrust with the weapon of self-knowledge. It is a double-edged weapon, but the only one which gives man the power to free himself from the dark forces preying on his nature. Only through understanding of one's own problems is it possible to overcome the fear of the irrational. In *The Shadow Line* the Captain is so understanding when Burns raves about the deceased commander, because he himself suspects the presence of some mysterious Power haunting the ship. And for the same reason the Captain in "The Secret Sharer" sympathizes with Legatt, whose emotions he himself shares.

Captain MacWhirr too has such moments of introspection, despite his unimaginative nature. In the solitude and darkness of the cabin, he speaks to himself, as if addressing another being stirred within his breast. The burden of command in a situation of danger becomes intolerable even to his feeble imagination. The senselessly destructive wrath of the gale causes not only overwhelming bodily fatigue, but also severe mental stress. It is sort of insidious fatigue that penetrates deep into a man's soul and makes him crave for peace. It also causes a man's mind to turn upon himself in aimless concentration. MacWhirr resists the temptation to allow the brute forces of nature to destroy him. But more sensitive men, like Jukes for instance, are apt to engage in do-nothing heroics in times of acute stress. The fury of the hurricane renders them indifferent and irresponsible. Had Jukes not had Captain MacWhirr on board, he would have faced the predicament of Lord Jim, who was also a victim of this sudden paralysis in a moment of danger, "the creeping paralysis of a hopeless outlook." [8]

The terror, perfidy and violence of the sea are a test of man's solidarity, and at the same time they enhance the isolation of the ship and its crew. An overdose of imagination as well as lack of it may add momentum to the forces of separation acting on board ship. The Captain in *The Shadow Line*, who combines imagination with the oppressing sense of his responsibility of command, is thus afflicted:

I was already the man in command. My sensations *could not be like those of any other man on board.* In that community I *stood, like a king in his country, in a class by myself.*[9]

Although the sea in Conrad's work is often shown as capable of betraying the ardor of youth, as a power that breaks the hearts of men, it is also described with love and tenderness as a source of inspiration and heroism for his protagonists. The sea, for all its immensity of indifference to man's fate, for all the hard knocks it deals the sailor, can still be a place of romance. Not so the jungle, whose concealed terrors produce a disintegrating influence on the white man. The jungle is seen by Conrad as a symbol of the savage in man, and, one is tempted to add, as a symbol of his isolation. The white man in the wilderness wages a double battle: against the destructive powers preying on his body as well as against forces undermining his moral integrity. Protected by law and police, the people in an organized civilized community live in fear of scandal, crime or insanity. They cannot understand the powers of darkness, for they never ask themselves

. . . what particular region of the first ages a man's untrammelled feet may take him into *by the way of solitude—utter solitude* without a policeman—by the wall of silence—utter silence, where no warning voice of a kind neighbor can be heard whispering of public opinion.[10]

Stripped of the refinements of civilization, man is left entirely to his own resources. He must fall back upon his inner strength, his power of devotion not to himself but to whatever obscure, back-breaking business he has in the wilderness. If his strength is sapped by the sheer physical destructiveness of the jungle or by his half-willing surrender to the mysterious forces of the savage tribe (or else if there is no strength in him at all), he is lost.

The theme of the white man's isolation and defeat by the force of the wliderness already appears in the first two novels of Conrad, *Almayer's Folly* (1895) and *An Outcast of the Islands* (1896). In the six years following the publication of the latter, this theme reappears in "An Outpost of Progress" (1898), "Heart of Darkness" (1899) and in *Lord Jim* (1900). Almayer's dream of wealth and power is wrecked when his daughter is claimed and won by the native warrior, Dain. One of the main causes of Willems's fall and death is his infatuation with the savage Aïssa. The fate of Lord Jim resembles that of Kurtz and Kayerts. He too perishes in the midst of a forest, destroyed by the revenge of a tribal chief. Yet this is a superficial resemblance, because Jim succumbs not to the dark powers of the wilderness but to the promptings of his own conscience. Still, *Lord Jim* shows a keen awareness of the white man's dilemma in keeping his integrity in alien surroundings. This is the main theme of "An Outpost of Progress" and "Heart of Darkness." The white man, stranded in the continent of black man, is destroyed physically and morally.

Carlier's and Kayerts' plight is very much like that of Kurtz, except that they have neither the opportunity nor the capability of finding the heart of darkness with its horror. But what they have to face is sufficient to kill them. They lose the battle for physical survival without much fight because they are totally unfitted for the struggle with the jungle. They are simple men, prisoners of their established routines of life. When they are set free from lifelong habits, they soon abandon their fixed standard of conduct. Plunged into the darkness of an immense forest, they live like blind men, understanding nothing and caring for nothing. Their moral breakdown is almost undistinguishable from physical exhaustion. Actually, it is the physical collapse (which comes as a result of the strangeness of environment) that causes the moral crises. Their discovery of themselves as "naked souls," bared of the accoutrements of their civilization, is fatal.

Kayerts' inability to see clearly makes him lose his self-control, which, in turn, leads him to the idea that life under the circumstances (after he had shot the unarmed Carlier) is more unbearable than death. The problem has assumed a moral aspect, but Kayerts does not long for atonement. His suicide implies that the peace of death is better than a life of moral decay and utter isolation—an implication made grim by the ironic image of the irreverent, swollen tongue thrust out at the Managing Director by the hanging corpse.

"An Outpost of Progress" anticipates "Heart of Darkness," where the symbolism is more distinct and the fall of the white men more significant because it is willed by Kurtz himself. A Kayerts (or a Carlier) cannot be imagined turning his back on civilization and setting his face towards the wilderness. Kurtz's betrayal of his Intended to the Heart of Darkness, and also his betrayal of his Western civilization reveal what thrilled and perplexed Marlow: the thought of the cannibal's humanity, the thought of his remote kinship with the savages. This dangerous idea will not be condoned by civilized society.

Like the Captain in "The Secret Sharer," Marlow identifies himself with a man who is lost. His search for Kurtz in the depths of the primeval forest, his interest in Kurtz's moral integrity, reflect (as in "The Secret Sharer") the quest for self-knowledge, which is found in all works of Conrad, where this spinner of yarns engages the attention of the silent audience, and in many others as well. The Captain in "The Secret Sharer," isolated by his secret, will arrive at more profound self-understanding after he has sounded the problems of Legatt and helped him. Marlow in *Lord Jim* is a wiser and perhaps a sadder man after his painstaking and painful efforts to penetrate Jim's motives and to restore the young man's self-confidence. Similarly, Marlow's purpose in "Heart of Darkness" is to explore his own soul by trying to understand why he is fascinated by Kurtz.

The mind of man, Marlow notes, is capable of anything, because it contains the past and the future alike. But though the wilderness, to use Marlow's own phrase, has patted him on the head, and has isolated him from his fellows, it has not totally severed his link with civilization. Marlow alone, among the members of the expedition, is aware of the true

nature of Kurtz's fall. In his attempts to retrieve Kurtz from
the jungle he ultimately frees himself from the momentary
spell the wilderness held over him. Marlow's ordeal of looking into the mad soul of Kurtz is like the latter's blind and
helpless struggle with himself. Both are subject to the same
temptation, but only Kurtz has reached the state of an incredible degradation. The potent suggestiveness and the
dreamlike quality of Kurtz's words shake Marlow profoundly, but he keeps his head though not his soberness. The fate
of Kurtz is, in a sense, a symbolic warning to Marlow to
beware of the danger of extreme isolation. Kurtz "had
kicked himself loose of the earth . . . he had kicked the very
earth to pieces. . . . He was alone . . .[11] This is the penalty
he must pay for having yielded to the dark powers of the
forest and to his own primitive emotions.

Marlow is fascinated, but not touched by the face of
the dying Kurtz. It seems to him that a veil (as symbolic
as the one in *The Rescue*) had been rent off Kurtz's ivory
face, disclosing to him the man's somber pride, his ruthless
power and his hopeless despair. Marlow, who has glanced
over the edge of the precipice, fully knows the meaning of
Kurtz's stare on his death-bed. He himself has withdrawn
from the abyss, not without some hesitation. Therein, he
adds, is the whole difference—in that moment of time, in
which he has crossed the threshold of the invisible. Marlow
could draw back because he sensed the danger in time, yet
his contact with the Heart of Darkness and, on the psychological plane, with the darkness of Kurtz's heart, has made
him no less an isolato than the object of his obscure loyalty.

After Kurtz's death he comes to Brussels, full of disgust
for its people who are intruders because they cannot possibly understand his state of mind. This consciousness of
special knowledge again isolates him from mankind. He
walks in the city, bitterly grinning at people, haunted by
the vision of Kurtz on the stretcher. The gloom of the jungle, and the beating of the drums are still vivid in his

imagination. When he brings this vision with him to Kurtz's
Intended, he realizes that he can never stop seeing that
eloquent phantom as long as he lives. The memory of Kurtz
is like a dream (or rather like a nightmare) which he can
share with nobody else. Kurtz's Intended is isolated by her
grief and her illusion of his integrity and greatness. Blinder
than the others who regard Kurtz as a mere madman, she
carries within her mind this illusion as Marlow harbors a
secret that cannot be divulged. Man must forever remain
shut within the shell of his own personality. The Captain in
"The Secret Sharer" also has his secret which sets him apart
from his crew. Marlow doubts whether his experiences can
ever be conveyed to his listeners. He has come to believe
that "we live as we dream—alone." [12]

CHAPTER IV

THE ANATOMY OF BETRAYAL

THE READER'S ETHICAL INTEREST in a work of imagination is as valid as his simple curiosity because a faithful account of life contains not only an excitement but also a moral. This view of Conrad, expressed in an essay on Guy de Maupassant,[1] is upheld by his practice. His work appeals to the eye and to the ear; there is the excitement of a "whodunit," the suspense of a thriller, the weirdness of a mystery story, the glamor and romance of a traveler's tale. But Conrad seems more concerned with the moral atmosphere of his fiction than with sheer exoticism which holds an appeal for the average reader. In fact, Conrad's technique of the restricted point of view, which to all appearances dispenses with the reader's curiosity to know what is going to happen in the end, at times defeats his dramatic intent and exasperates the unfortunate reader who is more interested in the story than in the Marlovian quest for truth.

Conrad rarely compromises with the reader, however. His professed desire to wield the magic wand that gives command over laughter and tears and makes people pause to look at the world of form and color is not the sum total of his artistic aims. What is equally (if not more) important to him is the general truth that underlies the action of his fictional world, and the moral complexion of life. This truth can be found in a conscious or subconscious search for reality, which often culminates in an ironic and tragic end.

The situations in which Conrad's protagonists find themselves are frequently beyond the pale of our daily lives. A white man is placed on the brim of a jungle, left at the mercy of savage natives. Unscrupulous adventurers set upon their innocent, unsuspecting victims. There are violent storms, dark plots, revolutions, intrigues, abductions, earthquakes, wars, duels and the horrors of an immense darkness. Conrad's outcasts face a mysterious and inclement universe, pervaded by a merciless logic for a futile purpose. It is an impersonally hostile world which they can never hope to understand. The most they can hope from life is some knowledge of themselves—that, generally, comes too late. The extent of the misfortunes that befall Conrad's heroes can be illustrated by the following table which shows how many of them are violently killed, commit suicide or otherwise destroy themselves in an act of self-sacrifice, die of disease or loneliness, go through a severe emotional crises or turn insane.

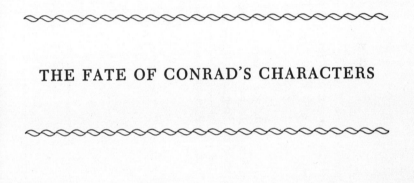

THE FATE OF CONRAD'S CHARACTERS

THE FATE OF CONRAD'S CHARACTERS

Some of Conrad's heroes pass through crises and ordeals during which they are on the point of despair, but they eventually emerge from their isolation. Their names are marked by an asterisk. The titles are arranged chronologically. The table includes all but two finished fictional works of Conrad (*Youth* and "The Black Mate"). The works in collaboration with Ford Madox Ford are not considered.

TITLE OF WORK	VIOLENTLY KILLED	COMMIT SUICIDE OR SACRIFICE THEMSELVES	DIE OF DISEASE OR OF LONELINESS	GO THROUGH SEVERE EMOTIONAL CRISIS (DESPAIR OR MELANCHOLY)	TURN INSANE
Almayer's Folly			Almayer	Almayer Nina Mrs. Almayer	
An Outcast of the Islands	Willems			Willems Mrs. Willems Babalatchi Aïssa Almayer	Aissa
Tales of Unrest "Karain"	Matara			Karain*	

"The Idiots"	Jean-Pierre Bacadou	Susan Bacadou		The Bacadous, Madame Levaille	
"An Outpost of Progress"	Carlier	Kayerts		Carlier, Kayerts	Kayerts
"The Return"				Alvan Hervey, Mrs. Hervey	
"The Lagoon"	Arsat's brother		Diamelen	Arsat	
Lord Jim	Brown, Lord Jim, Dain Waris	Jim, Capt. Brierly		Jim, Jewel, Doramin	
"Heart of Darkness"			Kurtz	Marlow*, Kurtz, Kurtz's Intended	Kurtz
"The End of the Tether"		Capt. Whalley		Capt. Whalley, Whalley's daughter	
"Amy Foster"			Yanko Goorall	Amy Foster	
"To-Morrow"			Hagberd	Bessie Carvil	
"Falk"				Falk*, Hermann's niece*	

TITLE OF WORK	VIOLENTLY KILLED	COMMIT SUICIDE OR SACRIFICE THEMSELVES	DIE OF DISEASE OR OF LONELINESS	GO THROUGH SEVERE EMOTIONAL CRISIS (DESPAIR OR MELANCHOLY)	TURN INSANE
Nostromo	Hirsch Nostromo	Decoud Dr. Monyg-ham	Teresa Viola	Nostromo, Decoud Dr. Monygham, Charles Gould, Emilia Gould, Linda, Giselle, Don Avellanos, Antonia Avellanos, Georgio Viola, Hirsch	Georgio Viola
The Mirror of the Sea "Tremolino"	Cesar			Dominic Gervoni* The "I" of the narrator*	
The Secret Agent	Mr. Verloc Stevie	Mrs. Verloc		Mrs. Verloc Comrade Tom Ossipon	
A Set of Six "Gaspar Ruiz"	Gaspar Ruiz	Erminia Gaspar Ruiz		Erminia Gaspar Ruiz	

"The Informer"	Sevrin	Sevrin Lady Amateur
"The Brute"	Maggie Colchester	The Captain* and the entire crew
"The Anarchist"		The Anarchist
"The Duel"		Armand D'Hubert* Feraud
"Il Conde"		The Count
Under Western Eyes	Razumov Victor Haldin	Razumov Nathalie Haldin
'Twixt Land and Sea. "A Smile of Fortune"		The Captain Alice Jacobus
"The Secret Sharer"		Legatt The Captain*
"Freya of the Seven Isles"	Freya Nelson	Freya Nelson Jasper Heemskirk Old Nelson

TITLE OF WORK	COMMIT SUICIDE OR SACRIFICE THEMSELVES	DIE OF DISEASE OR OF LONELINESS	GO THROUGH SEVERE EMOTIONAL CRISIS (DESPAIR OR MELANCHOLY)	TURN INSANE
Chance	Anthony	De Barral	Flora De Barral* De Barral Capt. Anthony*	
Victory	Lena Jones Ricardo	Heyst Lena	Heyst Lena	Jones
Within the Tides "The Planter of Malata"	Renouard		Renouard	
"The Partner"	Harry Dunbar	Stafford	Stafford	
"The Inn of the Two Witches"	Tom Corbin			
"Because of the Dollars"	Laughing Ann The Frenchman		Laughing Ann	

The Shadow Line			The young Captain* Burns
The Arrow of Gold			George*
			Doña Rita
			Ortega
			Capt. Blunt
The Rescue	Jaffir	Jörgenson	Lingard
			Mrs. Travers*
			Hassim
			Jaffir
			Mr. Travers*
The Rover	Peyrol	Peyrol	Réal*
	Michel		Arlette*
	Scevola		Scevola
Tales of Hearsay "Prince Roman"			Prince Roman*
"The Tale"	The Northman and his crew		The Commanding Officer
"The Warrior's Soul"	De Castel		De Castel
			Tomassov

117

With few exceptions, the characters listed in this table are isolatoes. It is not only the different methods of murder, mishap or suicide that account for variety in this gallery of unfortunates. It is perhaps Conrad's understanding of the diversity of solitude, of the multifariousness of human anguish, that turns his heroes into varied individuals, and draws them into the common orbit of isolation—a basic experience of their lives and of his own.

Conrad's lonely heroes are an affirmation of human solidarity. Man's isolation proves that no person with a conscience can live by himself. The hardened criminals, the half-wits—these *can* live alone, but theirs is a miserable existence. For men with even an elementary sense of right and wrong there is no escape from mankind, because there is no escape from themselves. No transgression against the principle of human solidarity remains unpunished—in Conrad's books, at any rate. The supreme sin, to Conrad, is failure to be loyal, which in its more extreme form is betrayal. Betrayal is to Conrad the crime of crimes, as fidelity is to him the virtue of virtues, and his books and stories are peopled with an astounding variety of traitors. It is not easy to classify them, but a clear distinction can be made between traitors who exhibit self-pity at their own weakness and their subsequent plight (Almayer, Willems, Kayerts) and the "sympathetic" traitors who are not only subject to a severe inner conflict resulting from their act of unfaithfulness, but who also inflict the punishment for it upon themselves. This latter kind includes men who long for redemption (Karain, Arsat, Lord Jim, Razumov, Nostromo, Lingard and others). A third type of traitor belongs in Conrad's crowded gallery of miscreants who are seldom interesting individuals in themselves, but only in so far as they demonstrate the blind and cruel forces affecting human destiny. These traitors have no remorse because they have no conscience. Their isolation is not less extreme but less painful.

That this theme of betrayal is of fundamental importance to Conrad can be seen from the fact that the two works which had given him the most trouble, *The Rescue* (begun in 1896 and completed in 1920) and *The Sisters* (given up in 1896) contain this *motif*. In the former Lingard becomes a traitor to the natives who trust him; the latter tells of Stephen's betrayal of home and parents. The first two novels of Conrad, *Almayer's Folly* and *An Outcast of the Islands*, are similarly stories of traitors. Almayer and Willems break the accepted moral code of their time. They break the white man's code. Each takes a woman of a different race only to find in her a total stranger. Willems, moreover, betrays his patron, Lingard. Almayer's lonely existence is a breach of human solidarity. Unable to live like a native, he tries to escape the real world by dreaming of wealth and his return to the Old World. But the Old World will not accept his daughter, Nina, nor does she want to go there. In his egotistic preoccupation with his reveries he ignores her feelings, scarcely regarding her as another human being, for Nina is to him not a young woman but a symbol of beauty and perfection, the idealized projection of his own self. She is the stimulus that drives him to seek gold, and through her he wishes to attain respectability which he cannot have with a Malay wife.

The dreams of his wife and daughter are quite different. Mrs. Almayer, who savagely hates her husband and the white race in general, yearns for revenge. Nina's greatest desire is to be united with her native lover Dain. She contemptuously discards her past, while Almayer desires to regain his. She feels no remorse at leaving her father, whose ambitions she does not understand, whose feelings are unknown to her. She is indifferent to her mother's hate and her thirst for revenge. The only thing this beautiful half-caste girl has in common with her mother is resentment against the city whites who humiliated her.

To Almayer Nina's love for a native means abject betrayal and the end to all his hopes. He makes two symbolic attempts to defy his love for Nina: he erases the traces of her footprints and burns his "folly"—the house he has built for her. Both attempts are as futile as his dreams. The pang of humiliation, the wounded vanity, above all, the great passion of one's life cannot be erased from the mind. The great passion turns into self-pity and a frantic desire to forget everything. He deludes himself with the idea that Nina is only a burden which he must shake off, when actually he is dying of the separation from her.

Willems's marital life is no better than that of Almayer's, except that Willems does not hate his wife but quietly detests her. Joanna's submission and the adulation of her relatives flatter his ego. Too much engrossed in the sense of self-importance to note the abyss spreading between them, Willems is completely taken unawares by Joanna's sudden manifestation of independence and hate for him. Already badly shaken by the discovery of his fraud, he reels under this blow. Like Jim, he must flee from his own kin in order to attempt rehabilitation in a place where he is not known. This is the hopeless flight of a hunted beast, not Jim's pursuit of an ideal of conduct.

He has betrayed Lingard and, through his infatuation with Aïssa, he has betrayed his race as well. Lingard is shocked at the cold-blooded treachery of his former protégé. "You are alone . . ." he says to Willems, "Nothing can help you. Nobody will. You are neither white nor brown. You have no color as you have no heart." [2] His passion for the savage woman can also be viewed as a symbol of his utter degradation, of his isolation in the wilderness. Aïssa's "somber gaze" fits well into a picture of the great solid and somber trees of the jungle. As in "Heart of Darkness," the primeval forest becomes the symbol of the implacable destiny that closes in upon man.

The awakening from his love spell makes Willems even lonelier than he was before. In Aïssa he can see now his own cowardice and his sinful nature. His irresolute dreams of rescue are mingled with attacks of hysterical fear. He can no longer rely on his previous conviction that he would muddle through—somehow. Willems's patron and protector is now an ominous and hostile figure. The dreams of greatness contrast cruelly with the sordidness of his downfall. He hates himself as much as he hates Aïssa. Immobile and tense, this passionate, savage woman is a constant reminder of his failure. Ironically, the woman who was to be his refuge from the world's troubles, turns out to be destiny's punishment for his betrayals—of his company, of Lingard, of his wife, his class, and, finally, of Aïssa herself.

She is also an outcast and a traitor. To the white people she must always be the contemptible pariah and her own tribe looks on her as a deserter. Like Almayer, and so many other protagonists of Conrad, she is isolated by her consuming passion which blots out everything else from her mind. Willems's love is to her the everlasting thing, and he the *one* man in the whole world, but his actions and emotions are beyond her reach. Willems's sudden transformation from a great man into a pitiful weakling has a merely personal meaning to her—the possible loss of her lover. His hatred is as incomprehensible to her as his love, and it evokes in turn bewilderment, apathy and despair. His momentary decision to seek forgetfulness in that which he hates, despises and fears, is not the comeback for which Aïssa has been yearning. On the contrary, it makes him more miserable than ever and only enhances his solitude. These two human beings in each other's arms, yet so utterly torn apart, are a pathetic sight. Their isolation has reached the limit.

Those two, *surrounded each by the impenetrable wall* of their aspirations, were *hopelessly alone*, out of sight, out of earshot of each other; each the centre of dissimilar and distant horizons; standing *each on a different earth, under a different sky*.[3]

Fate has brought them together only to destroy them. This is the final blow which the wilderness deals the guilty Willems.

Not only the major characters in *Almayer's Folly* and *An Outcast of the Islands* are isolatoes; the "supporting cast" are also pariahs, as often as not governed by greed, hate or violent passion. Thus, Joanna is as much a stranger to her husband as the wild Aïssa; Nina's tortuous love for Dain borders on despair and suicide. There is an impassable barrier between her and Almayer whom she regards as a member of an alien and hostile race. Taminah is an outcast, Omar an exile; Lakamba lives in isolation among his wives and retainers. Even nature itself in this world of inescapable loneliness—the high seas and the dark forests, is a solitary exile.

In the Author's Note to *Tales of Unrest* Conrad notes that the *motif* of the first story, "Karain: A Memory," is almost identical with that of the last tale, "The Lagoon," which was written two years after the composition of *An Outcast of the Islands*. The mood and the method in Conrad's first two books and these two tales are the same. The identical *motif* is betrayal, followed by gnawing remorse and a destructive sense of isolation. Karain cannot escape from the ghost of his friend, whom he has betrayed and killed; nor can Arsat (in "The Lagoon") forget his beloved brother, whom he has abandoned for the sake of a woman. Both men are nearly driven to madness by the haunting memory of their acts.

Karain's deliverance from his suffering is ironic, for it is effected by dint of a white man's compassionate lie. The white man's magic box seems to the poor fugitive to contain a vast power over the living and the dead; and because he believes in its charm Karain is relieved from the fear of outer darkness. He has regained his peace of mind by trusting an illusion.

Arsat is not so fortunate. He cannot forget his action.

He left his brother to die among enemies while he paddled to safety with Diamelen, the girl he took away from the Ruler's Court. Crushed by a feeling of guilt, he is doomed to the anguish of utter loneliness, finding some relief perhaps in the telling of his sad tale to the white man.

This anguish of being alone is shared by Yanko Goorall and Prince Roman, the only two undisguised Poles in Conrad's fiction. Yanko is a' humble mountaineer who leaves his native shores in search of a better future, and turns into "a lost stranger, helpless, incomprehensible. . . .⁴ He is totally unprepared for his ordeal. This innocent adventurer has committed no crime save being different from the people in a Kentish or Sussex village, whose deep-seated hostility toward the outlandish looks and the ways of strangers make him a despised pariah.

Ah! He was different; innocent of heart, and full of good will, which nobody wanted, this castaway, that, like a man transplanted into another planet, was separated by an immense space from his past and by an immense ignorance from his future.⁵

Yanko's isolation is enhanced by the company of Amy, the girl he married, who is a very dull creature, barely tolerated by the people in the village. In the beginning Amy seems to be his savior—the only friendly soul in a menacing world. But when he falls ill and feverish Amy deserts him, frightened out of the house by his frantic supplications for water, which he utters in his native tongue. Instead of finding a new land of future, this pathetic young foreigner is "cast out mysteriously by the sea to perish in the supreme disaster of loneliness and despair." ⁶ No human being has understood him and his wife forsakes him at the moment he needs her most. He has evoked no pity in the dwellers of the Eastbay shores, nor has he left any marks on Amy's mind. His memory disappears from her dull brain as a shadow traverses a white screen.

Even his name is pathetic. Yanko is the Polish *Janku*—
the vocative of *Janek* which is the diminutive of *Jan* (John).
Why does Yanko give this form of his name to the strangers
in England? Obviously because he is haunted by the memory of his native village where everybody called him in a
familiar way. Perhaps he is thus trying to cling to his Polish
identity. It is one of Yanko's several attempts to retain
the ties with his homeland. And it is the only one which
goes undetected and unsuspected. His solitary singing in
the fields, his dancing in the tavern and his slavic manner-
isms are misunderstood by the people of Brenzett. It is
indeed poor consolation to Yanko Goorall that his son was
called Johnny by Amy Foster, which means little John.

Prince Roman, the other Pole of Conrad's fiction, has
little in common with Yanko Goorall except, perhaps, his
being miserable, too. Both men were suddenly struck by
misfortune, but there is a great difference in their respective situations. Prince Roman could not have prevented
the death of his beloved wife any more than Yanko could
have stopped the storm that cast him out into an alien land.
Yet Prince Roman's participation in the struggle of the
Polish patriots against the Russian oppressors was an act
of deliberate choice on his part. It was dictated by his conscience not by his despair.

Since Prince Roman is the only character in Conrad's
fiction to speak openly about the plight of Poland, and,
moreover, one that is based on Conrad's recollection of his
youth, it is noteworthy that he is one of the few of Conrad's
isolatoes who succeed in overcoming their isolation. At first,
the death of his wife causes Prince Roman to become indifferent to the fate of his fellow beings. They simply do not
exist for him. Like Almayer grieving over his daughter or
Willems bemoaning his bad luck, he is a lost man. But the
sight of his countryside and the example of his countrymen
in arms make him recover from his state of isolation. He
plunges into the struggle with the quixotery of a Lord Jim,

a George or a Lingard. He resembles Jim more than the others in putting his honor above everything else, and in realizing the moral bond that exists between him and his country, as Jim recognized the moral bond that demanded courage and sacrifice of him. The young recluse has turned into a man devoted to public welfare.

This moral transformation is a familiar theme in Polish literature. Prince Roman's change of heart, to cite two examples, is very similar to that of Robak (the adventurer turned priest, in Adam Mickiewicz's great epic poem, *Pan Tadeusz*), and Kmicic (in Henryk Sienkiewicz's *The Deluge*). Both Robak and Kmicic are at first concerned only with their loves and adventures, but later turn into model patriots, ready to give their lives for Poland. Prince Roman suffers a great deal and returns from exile, totally deaf. One cannot help wondering whether this handicap is coincidental with the historical fact reported in Conrad's story, or whether it has also symbolic significance. For, in a sense, deafness is symbolic punishment for Prince Roman, as it is for Razumov. The former has been deaf to his countrymen's cry for help. Now that he has come back to his people he must be separated from them by a wall of silence. The latter is mutilated by the anarchists who shatter his eardrums after he confesses his treason.

When Prince Roman appears before the Military Commission, the judges hopefully wait for words of penitence from the young man. Everything has been done to give him an opportunity of winning his freedom. But the Prince shows neither humility nor regret at his past behavior. He defies the offer of clemency and declares in writing, to provide the jury with tangible proof of his beliefs, that he has joined the national rising from conviction. To submit to the mercy of those whom he hates and despises would amount to moral degradation and a loss of honor without which life has no meaning. Like de Castel, the French officer in "The Warrior's Soul," Prince Roman realizes that the loss of all faith and courage is worse than death. He prefers slave labor or death to the empty existence of a sycophant at the Tsar's court. Although the Prince does not suffer from a sense of guilt, like Jim and Razumov, he resembles them in his voluntary acceptance of punishment for his transgression.

The act of self-sacrifice which has a purifying effect upon man, and which, moreover, reveals to man the ideal conception of his own personality, is found throughout Conrad's work. Lord Jim, Brierly and Razumov, to mention a few, have no true knowledge of themselves. When the meaning of their true selves dawns upon them, they seek death as a solution to their problems. In each case the moral censure comes from the man himself. Jim must give his life for the life of Dain, whose trust he has betrayed. Brierly's verdict in Jim's case discloses to him the hitherto unsuspected weakness of his own character. The conviction that he would not have acted differently had he been in Jim's place, exposes the flimsiness of his professed courage and prowess, and destroys his reason for living. He has identified himself with Jim, and since he punishes the young man for what may have been his own crime, he must also mete out punishment to himself, symbolically jumping into the sea—as Jim did.

Razumov, the hero of *Under Western Eyes*, goes through the same process of self-torture and self-sacrifice. Like Raskolnikov, he is a lonely student, preoccupied with moral and political issues. A bastard son of a nobleman, without family or friends, Razumov regards the national past of Russia as his real parent. The student revolutionaries reject that past, and therefore are his adversaries. Ironically, it is to him that Haldin comes with a plea for help, after killing a government official. Razumov betrays the fugitive revolutionist to the police—an act which turns him into a reluctant police agent. Henceforth, he will spy on the revolutionaries in Geneva. His sense of guilt grows more acute when he falls in love with Haldin's sister, Nathalie. Razumov (whose Russian name *razum* means reason) argues with himself morbidly until he reaches the conclusion that he must deliver himself into the hands of the revolutionaries and confess his guilt in order to wash away Haldin's blood. He does this at the time when nobody can prove his betrayal, hoping to regain his moral freedom.

Lord Jim and *Under Western Eyes* are studies of the split personality. Jim and Razumov have an *alter ego* of their consciousness, which they hold responsible for their failures and betrayals. Jim's attitude of forgiveness toward Gentleman Brown can be explained by his sympathetic identification of himself with the ruffian; he cannot condemn the outlaw without condemning himself. Similarly, in *Under Western Eyes* Razumov's double is Haldin, the student revolutionist. Razumov has a clearer understanding of, his position than Jim. "In giving Victor Haldin up," he confesses, "it was myself after all, whom I have betrayed most basely." [7]

He and Jim are spiritual masochists. They suffer from fears of abandonment, neglect or rejection. Against this, there is a strong aggressive reaction, with fear of counter-attack. The masochist wants to be hurt, and thus to be forgiven, thus to escape loneliness. The Western professor of foreign languages states Razumov's condition with the impartiality of a medical diagnosis when he compares Razumov to a man stabbing himself and then turning the knife in the wound.

The confessions of Jim to Marlow, and of Razumov to Nathalie, bear a distinct resemblance to Raskolnikov's self-abnegation before Sonya. The confession is extremely painful in each case, but it constitutes at the same time a source of relief—in the moral sense. Actually, these men never talk to anybody but themselves. They need a sympathetic audience because it helps them in clarifying their problem.

The confession of one individual to another is not

enough to ensure moral redemption. The culprit must also pass the ordeal of confession and admission of guilt at a public forum. Jim undergoes two such trials: at the court-room, after his desertion of the *Patna,* and in the court-yard of the chief Doramin. Razumov, not satisfied with Nathalie's compassion, can win his spiritual freedom by the typically Russian confession to an assembly of anarchists. The period of self-torture has culminated in an act of self-sacrifice through which man attains spiritual regeneration. Jim has a great deal in common with Dr. Monygham in *Nostromo.* Although he can plead the extenuating circum-stances of having betrayed his friends under torture, he is as morbidly engaged in the struggle for the dogma of con-science, as is Jim. Because he cannot forgive himself for his betrayal, he must at least know the secret of Nostromo's incorruptibility. After his betrayal, Dr. Monygham's life is a ceaseless attempt to redeem himself in the eyes of his people. He purifies himself morally by becoming a traitor in the cause which he serves. He undertakes to do the dirty work, and finds comfort in it.

To do these things in the character of a traitor was abhorrent to his nature and terrible to his feelings. He had *made that sacrifice in a spirit of abasement.*[8]

He can do everything because the exalted spirit of self-sacrifice has taken possession of his soul. This idea of atone-ment and suffering often occurs in Dostoyevsky. When Sonya learns the terrible truth about Raskolnikov, she un-hesitatingly decides that they must suffer together. They must go to prison and atone for the sin. Porfiry Petrovich tells Raskolnikov that he regards him as a man who would smile at his torturer if only he has found faith or God. Murder or betrayal abase man. To expiate the crime man must undergo more self-abasement. But Raskolnikov's hu-miliation before Sonya elevates him spiritually because he thereby pays tribute to all suffering mankind. The legal trial is only part of the proceedings. What matters is the trial of Raskolnikov by Raskolnikov himself.

The act of self-sacrifice is not necessarily caused by a transgression. The heroine of *Victory* is an innocent girl who was born on the wrong side of the tracks. An outcast in the world, Lena clings desperately to Heyst—the first kind and chivalrous man she has met. She prefers death to being deserted by her lover, yet she is aware, no less than Heyst, of the moral imperfection in their relationship. She hopes to achieve a complete union with him by suffering supremely for his sake, by an act of absolute sacrifice. Heyst, too, wishes to take the brunt of the sacrifice upon himself, leaving *her* out completely. He understands perfectly their isolated condition. "Never were such a lonely two out of the world, my dear!"[9] he says to Lena. Even their sacrifice for each other must be done in duplicity, which keeps them apart. Heyst acknowledges his responsibility for Lena, but he prefers to make a passive offering of his own life to the putting up of violent resistance against the bandits. This gesture, genuine though it may be, is the natural outcome of his morbid egotism, for it completely disregards Lena's feelings. He fails to understand how much *he* means to her.

Heyst's philosophy gets more and more muddled. Although he at one time observes, with an air of wisdom, that diplomacy without force in the background is but a rotten reed to lean upon, he would use neither the crowbar, nor his great physical strength to defend his own life and the woman who has become so dear to him. He has lived so long within himself, renouncing mankind and its experiences, that he has lost the will to live. He cannot lift a finger to fight Jones and his fellow bandits because he does not know *how* to defend himself. He is incapable of dealing with the realities of ordinary human existence. In a sense, he is not fully alive.

Heyst's isolated island offers no protection from life

and its evil; nor does D'Hubert's country retreat (in "The Duel") shield him from the pursuit by the irrational Feraud. Patusan cannot save Jim from the sudden but inevitable intrusion of Gentleman Brown, and the security of the Count's ivory tower (in "Il Conde") is shattered by the fierce *Cavaliere*. The moral that can be derived from these situations is this: when man is made to face the evil of the human soul and its primordial wilderness, he usually recognizes a certain degree of affinity with it. That is why the haunted and persecuted isolatoes cannot wholeheartedly condemn the person or power responsible for their misfortunes, lest they also condemn themselves. However, they can and do destroy themselves. The renunciation of common experiences is, in psychological terms, a kind of self-murder. Heyst subconsciously drives himself to death, for there is nothing to keep him on this earth. The diabolical bandits, who have come to take Lena away, hardly exist for him.

Decoud's predicament is similar. Unable to fall back on any religious, moral, or political dogma (which is man's link with the outside world), he disintegrates morally, for his life has been robbed of its sense of reality. Involvement in politics, in a love affair, even in displaying his own cynicism—those were the things that made life worth while. The brief existence on a lonely island, however, is more than he can endure because it reveals his own emptiness.

Decoud's suicide is a confirmation of his spiritual death. This brilliant Costaguanero of the boulevards dies from solitude and want of self-confidence. Like Ivan Karamazov, he is destroyed by his own skepticism. Suicide is the only solution of his moral dilemma. Yet his last moment is also the first moral sentiment of his life which, he finally admits to himself, has been misdirected.

Conrad often views death as the absolute sacrifice, the supreme moment of a man's life. To Willems death reveals for the first time the joy and the beauty of sunshine. To

Almayer it can only spell a sudden freedom from his anguish, for he was able to forget at last. The difference between the death of an Almayer and the end of a Jim or a Razumov is that the former seeks only escape and relief from pain, while the latter crave for self-knowledge and self-fulfilment, and meet death almost ecstatically.

Peyrol (in *The Rover*) dies smiling at his visions, gladly giving his life for the happiness of Réal and Arlette. His voluntary sacrifice is also a means of redeeming his good name as a Frenchman, after a life of turbulent roving over the seas. At last he has a chance to show his devotion to duty.

Captain Whalley (in "The End of the Tether") sacrifices himself for his daughter's happiness. But this simple and melodramatic story has also another level of meaning. Captain Whalley fails to reveal his blindness while responsible for the ship's safety. This is a betrayal of the ethics of his profession, for which he must pay. The last thoughts of Captain Whalley show a preoccupation with moral values. He realizes that for his daughter's sake he has almost committed a grave crime. His world has turned into a dark waste, and Whalley can see no reason why he should continue to live.

Of course, not all protagonists of Conrad are devoted to exalted ideals of conduct. For example, there is no moral crisis or moral quality in Willems's end. To him death is an intense sensual experience—nothing more. The supreme moment is the realization of the delights of sunshine, of the physical act of breathing and of feeling things. His life culminates in the glare of the sun, in the taste of salt in his mouth, and the falling curtain of darkness. How differently Lord Jim feels when he faces his executioner, with a proud and unflinching glance, certain of having achieved an extraordinary success. His act of self-sacrifice has set him free from his past failure, and has given him the power he had dreamed of—to be master of himself. He has lost all men's confidence for the second time in his life. His surrender to Doramin is a rebellion against the dark powers that, in his belief, have caused him to fail twice.

Razumov, like Jim (and also like Almayer), yearns not for the peace that comes with oblivion but for the peace which man attains when he learns the truth about himself. His confession to Miss Haldin will bring him the object of his search: "You were appointed to undo the evil by making me *betray myself back into* truth and peace." [10] That her brother, Victor, turns out to be not only his victim but also his savior may seem a somewhat perverse way of thinking. After all, Razumov has betrayed Victor Haldin and has sent him to the gallows. How can he regard this man as his personal redeemer, and express his gratitude to him? But as Razumov has always occupied himself with his own ego and nothing else, he finds nothing wrong with this logic. To him, as to Jim and other romantics of Conrad, his own feelings and, particularly, his own estimate of himself, are of paramount importance.

Razumov declares:

. . . to-day I made myself free from falsehood, from remorse—independent of every human being on this earth. [11]

Jim could have uttered these words with equal pertinence. Both men reach a point where they have done with their lives. And Razumov, like Jim, is willing to die because this means an escape from an ignominious life of falsehood. Punishment for their transgression is the final epiphany to Lord Jim and Razumov. It reveals to them the essence of living, the moral truth. It is their spiritual regeneration, their ultimate redemption.

Not so Nostromo's death, which strikes him after he has collapsed spiritually. He is even more shaken by his first defeat than Jim, for while Jim only dreamed of achievement, Nostromo, the darling of the crowds, has lived in the aura of men's adoration. He is not prepared to deal with any crisis except in terms of physical survival. When Decoud commits suicide, Nostromo is faced with a moral decision for the first time in his life. Decoud shot himself, capsizing the boat and taking four ingots of silver to weigh down his body. Nostromo cannot explain his disappearance, and he is baffled by the missing ingots. But since he is the only other man to whom the silver treasure was entrusted, he can no longer return it without being charged with the theft of the missing ingots—an accusation which he cannot disprove. Thus, the only solution seems to be to take the whole treasure, which he does as the course of events in the war-torn republic of Costaguana plays into his hands.

The silver, however, has brought him bad luck. The crime is a malignant growth which consumes his life. It has turned his former courage and magnificence into sham. The very fact that men do not generally suspect his treachery troubles the fiery Capataz de Cargadores. Decoud has betrayed him, and "a man betrayed," he tells himself, "is a man destroyed . . . Destroyed!" [12] This statement is equally true in regard to Nostromo himself, when he turns traitor by hiding the treasure. He commits a kind of suicide, for he has destroyed that by which he has lived. He is tormented by fears and humiliated by the necessity of acting by stealth. Suddenly the world is without faith and courage, and universal dissolution appears near. Plunged into the darkness of falsehood, he now fears lest a ray of light be directed against it and shine upon his disgrace. The only solid thing left is the treasure of silver which he has buried on a deserted island, but this too, he finds out, is sham.

The sense of guilt weighs heavily upon him. In a pose recalling Macbeth he anxiously watches his hands for the stain of the cursed metal. But though Nostromo looks suicide deliberately in the face, he never loses his head. He

understands that there is no escape, but unlike Jim, Razumov, Brierly and Decoud, he is incapable of imagining
himself dead. He is possessed too strongly by the reality
of his own existence to grasp the notion of finality. Seeking
the relief of confession, Nostromo trusts his secret to Giselle, one of the Viola sisters who love him. His confession,
however, is not complete for he does not tell her about
the hiding spot of the treasure. He has not fully compre-
hended the nature of his betrayal, therefore he cannot regain moral freedom. It is tragic irony that he should be
killed by the father of Giselle with whom he is planning
a new life.

The whole truth must out before he dies, and the person to learn it is Doña Emilia who does not wish to hear
the story of his betrayal. But now it is too late for absolution. The magnificent Capataz de Cargadores, who has
lived his own life on the assumption of unbroken fidelity,
rectitude, and courage, dies broken-hearted and in moral
solitude which, Conrad asserts, no human being can bear
steadily without losing his mind.

Moral solitude may lead to destruction without causing madness. Decoud, who has detached himself from an
environment which he despises, without acquiring a saving
credo, suffers from intellectual isolation. Heyst regards
himself as the aloof observer of life, and will not get involved in action unless prompted by a sudden impulse of
kindness, which is inconsistent with his own philosophy.
Decoud observes the world and himself with an air of
amused disgust. Nothing escapes his scathing irony, not
even his own skepticism.

This philosophy irrevocably alienates them from mankind—a transgression for which many of Conrad's heroes
are punished by death. Humanity is bound by an *invincible conviction of solidarity* that knits together the loneliness of innumerable hearts."[13] He that breaks the law of
human solidarity finds himself in a moral desert and is

doomed to perdition. He who worships nothing but nature and reason discovers that in order to doubt one must have an opposing belief, that, in other words, man cannot live without a world of other men and their activity.

Decoud learns this truth when, after three days of total isolation on an island, he begins to doubt his own existence. From a mere outward condition of living solitude has become for him a state of soul in which neither irony nor skepticism have a meaning. His individuality disintegrates so swiftly because there is neither faith to hold it together nor sustaining illusion of an independent existence.

Similarly, in his fine detachment Heyst has lost the habit of asserting himself. Not that he wants the moral or physical courage of self-assertion. But he lacks the ability to make a decision in a critical moment of his life, which comes naturally to the unreflecting man. Conrad is an avowed enemy of the intellect:

Thinking is the great enemy of perfection. The habit of profound reflection, I am compelled to say, is the most pernicious of all the habits formed by the civilized man.[14]
[Moreover] . . . nothing humanly great—great, [I mean] as affecting a whole mass of lives—has come from reflection.[15]

One is tempted to ask whether Conrad grants an independent existence, or the illusion of such an existence, to the unspeculative men of action rather than to the introspective dreamers and adventurers. The reader of Conrad will note that the habit of profound reflection is not more pernicious than, say an idealized concept of personal honor or vanity. Nostromo, for example, whom nobody could suspect of being an intellectual, becomes a victim of his disenchanted vanity. Jim certainly does not fall prey to his powers of speculation. It seems that Conrad's wrath against the intellect does not prevent him from exposing the simple-minded men of action to the same dangers that beset his intellectuals. The McWhirrs and the Willemses, no less than the Heysts, the Decouds and the Marlows, may be subject to the state of extreme isolation. It is not surprising that Conrad, the intellectual with a tortuous memory, prefers the simplicity of a McWhirr to the complexity of a Heyst. But it is obvious that Conrad must create both kinds of men, for he himself lived a double life—as sailor and thinker. Many were the moments when he felt, in his own words, "broken up—and broken in two—disconnected." [16] And, surely, the reader will not take his negation of reflection too seriously. What he meant was that reflection unaccompanied by the spark of a great human emotion may be fruitless or destructive, which is largely true. Science is a product of profound thinking, but science without some humane principle guiding its use may indeed become pernicious, as our present history only too sadly illustrates.

Where man is not an isolato from the start, through irremediable circumstances of birth or ill-fortune, he must take the test of solitude. Only a few can break through it and return into the solidarity of their social group. Most of Conrad's isolatoes, however, are alone even before fate has struck them unawares, and all of them must suffer the penalty, the guilty and the innocent alike. Lord Jim is a solitary dreamer *before* the *Patna* incident; and Razumov of *Under Western Eyes*

. . . was as lonely in the world as a man swimming in the deep sea. The word Razumov was the mere label of a solitary individuality. There were no Razumovs belonging to him anywhere. His closest parentage was defined in the statement that he was a Russian.[17]

Decoud and Heyst are isolated from the moment they are introduced to the reader, and they never succeed in fulfilling their lives. Decoud's cosmopolitanism posing as intellectual superiority is a manifestation of his separate-

ness. He is neither a Frenchman nor a Spaniard nor a Costaguanero—a man without a country, an idle cumberer of
the globe. His passion for Antonia will make of him a
Blanco journalist but not a patriot. His skepticism and
cynicism remain unbroken. He is the dilettante in life,
fearing the power of conviction because as soon as it becomes effective it turns into a sort of destructive dementia.
Conviction is faith of some sort, and to live without any
faith, without any ties, is to accept the verdict of impend-
ing doom. Heyst believes a man to be lost if he forms a
tie. He is a man of universal scorn and unbelief. He is also
"the most detached of creatures in this earthly captivity,
the veriest tramp of this earth, an indifferent stroller going
through the world's bustle." [18] He claims that the world
for the wise is nothing but an amusing spectacle. The view
that the universe is not ethical at all but purely spectacular leads to the vision of the immense indifference of
things, which swallows poor Decoud and other victims of
disenchantment and solitude. It also results in a fatal
denial of reality. Heyst, like that mad hidalgo of La Mancha, wants to escape from the intolerable reality of things.
He naïvely trusts that the world will leave him in peace.
But life catches up with him and subjects his philosophy
to a crucial test. What ensues is the familiar tragedy, somewhat mitigated by the moral triumph of Lena before her
death. Heyst's principles fail him when, in a moment of
inexplicable (to him) compassion for poor Morrison, he
offers him his help and thus forms what he considers a
disastrous tie. Heyst's entire attitude towards life has collapsed before the reality of Lena's love for him. In the
end, a new light has dawned upon him and he cries out:
"Woe to the man whose heart has not learned while young
to hope, to love—and to put its trust in life." [19]

Heyst broke the law of human solidarity in fearing to
take the full risk of humanity. The test, which invariably
comes to the Conradian protagonist, reveals to him his

helplessness in dealing with the problems of life. Despite his physical prowess and the intrepidity of his character, Heyst is unable to protect Lena and himself from the three ruffians. Like Jim, but for different reasons, he is paralyzed when action is necessary.

The invasion of his isolated island by the three evil "messengers" of the outside world is a phenomenon which he regards with a sense of fatality. The bandits, who come to the island with a clear intent to murder him and extort from him the treasure they believe he possesses, do not arouse his temper. By this time Heyst has refined every-thing away—anger, indignation, scorn itself. Nothing re-mains but disgust. His subsequent loss of his revolver is a symbol of the loss of his will-power. He is totally incapa-ble of defending himself because he has failed to accept the world as it is. Even Lena, the human being who is so close to him, is mysterious and unreal to him.

That girl was to him like a script in an unknown language, or even more simply mysterious, like any writing to the illiterate. [it was] . . . the physical and *moral sense* of imperfection of their relations—a sense . . . which made her so vague, so *elusive* and illusory, a promise that could not be embraced and held.[20]

The lovers are total strangers to each other. The atmos-phere of utter wilderness is not conducive to mutual un-derstanding. It is doubtful whether Heyst and Lena could have attained a real closeness of spirit under any circum-stances. They are set apart from each other by the vast difference in the surroundings from which they stem and, moreover, both are suffering from hypersensitiveness. They are separated from each other by the gloom of their own making. Their sensitiveness is actually an extreme form of egoism. Lena is too much absorbed in *her* desire to sacri-fice herself at the altar of *her* love, to perceive that Heyst simply does not know how to express himself. Therefore she does not do the one sensible thing under the circumstances: she fails to warn her lover of the danger to which she is exposed. Instead, she puts the blame on herself for having inadvertently brought the trouble upon Heyst, and resorts to duplicity in order to defend her lover. Lena is too simple-minded to understand Heyst's ideas, and too much in love with him to rationalize his behavior. He seems to her "too *self-contained,* and as if *shut up in a world of his own.*" [21] Heyst suffers from a trouble with which she has nothing to do. She cannot understand the kind of existence which he offers her, nor can she fathom his pessimism. His uprootedness, Heyst admits, is an unnatural state of existence, which breeds the "mystic wound" from which both these unfortunates suffer.

This mystic wound or, as some would have it, the cosmic nostalgia, is the theme of *Chance.* Here there are also two isolatoes, a man and a woman, whom fate has brought together, and who are unable to attain mutual understanding although they are deeply in love with each other. Captain Anthony is as chivalrous and quixotic as Axel Heyst, and, one might add, as inexperienced in love matters. Flora, like Lena, is a social outcast who finds in her lover the only support in a world which struck at her with devastating ferocity. Both girls have a peculiarity of temperament (one of several isolating factors in their lives), which breeds in them a morbid feeling of fear and insecurity. They suffer from a strong inferiority complex, which Lena overcomes through her sacrifice and Flora with the help of chance.

Flora's redemption is real, but Lena's is only an illusory belief that she has saved Heyst by taking the knife from Ricardo. Although Heyst understands neither her action nor her emotions in the last moments of her life, she believes that she has won him at last. Looking at the dying girl Heyst remains absolutely idle. Lena is triumphant because she knows that there is no one else who could have made this sacrifice for Heyst. She has won her victory over death. But Heyst is beaten. He can only curse his fastidious soul, "which even at that awful moment kept the true cry of love from his lips in its *infernal mistrust of all life.*" [22] Yet Heyst, too, has achieved his redemption, for Lena's death has finally made him realize the danger and the absurdity of his philosophy. Lena's "tremendous achievement" in self-sacrifice has made this recluse of a man a true lover who will never forget her image. The tie with Lena, which, like everything else, has seemed vague and indistinct is now real; so real, indeed, that he cannot go on living because he cannot stand his thoughts before Lena's dead body. This denial of life without Lena and her love is Heyst's affirmation of spiritual values. Before Lena's sacrifice the only feelings he knew were contempt or amusement. Now, for the first time in his life, Heyst speaks with an accent of unconcealed despair. Paradoxically enough, his suicide is the ultimate manifestation of Heyst's redemption: it symbolizes his return to humanity.

CHAPTER V

THE PERFIDIOUS HAND
OF FATE

There are in life events, contacts, glimpses, that
seem brutally to bring all the past to a close.
There is a shock and a crash, as of a gate flung
to behind one by the perfidious hand of fate.[1]

In *Victory*, as in *Chance*, everything is
subject to the unexpected turns of destiny. By sheer chance
Lena meets Heyst. Inexplicable fate brings the three ruffians to Samburan. The sudden appearance of Davidson
a moment after Lena has been shot is a *deus ex machina*
climax. It has no connection whatever with the plot of
the novel. The melodramatic structure of *Chance* is less
noticeable because it contains a consistently narrated story
of one man's fall and the consequences it produced. The
reasons for de Barral's fall were not only circumstances;
they were, in fact, his poor judgment, his lack of imagination if not plainly his stupidity in matters of finance. But
even in *Chance*, where the narrative climbs to a dramatic
climax with Flora's attempted suicide, Conrad interposes
events which do not fit within the dramatic structure of
the novel. The death of Captain Anthony, for instance,

141

serves no dramatic purpose. He drowns in a collision several years after his reconciliation with Flora, only to give young Powell a chance for a successful courtship of the luckless widow. Anthony's exit is, in fact, an anti-climax. The whole thing reads like an afterthought but, on the other hand, structural weakness is often compensated by a symbolic pattern. Conrad's method is to all intents and purposes an anticipation of modern fiction techniques. The world of James Joyce and Virginia Woolf is also conveyed in seemingly disconnected pictures which do not fit within the arbitrary rules of drama, nor within any other rules for that matter. It is governed by a symbolic rather than a dramatic consistency.

The melodrama of *Victory* presents such a world. The book is poorly constructed, but it has a singular symbolic felicity. The sudden appearance of the knife-wielding Ricardo, the women-hating Jones and the savage Pedro, is a grimly symbolic retribution for Heyst's and Lena's guilt. The three evil messengers represent the world at its worst, closing in upon Heyst's retreat. Heyst suspects that a fatal destiny hangs over his and Lena's life, and that they are helpless "slaves of *this infernal surprise* which has been sprung on [us] by—shall I say *fate?*" Lena wishes to know whether the trouble on the island "was not *a sort of punishment.*" Heyst wonders at her words. "A *sort of retribution* from an angry Heaven?" he asks in complete surprise, and is profoundly moved by her whisper that theirs has been a *"guilty life."* [2] But the Heystian manner prevents him from understanding her meaning fully. As usual, he is playful and ironic. And since he considered himself a lost man already, he can indulge in his delicate raillery.

The rapid succession of unexpected events symbolizes the central theme of the novel (and the central idea in the whole body of Conrad's fiction) that betrayal of human solidarity and a breach of faith are always punished, that the price of atonement is death.

The dramatic looseness of *Victory, Chance* and *Lord Jim* is an excellent device for the writer to convey the instability of the world. A dramatically consistent plot means careful construction on the part of the writer. But life is the reverse of a planned existence. It is an endless chain of dull events broken by unexpected shocks. The end of Conrad's dramatic novel, like that of Proust's *A la recherche du temps perdu* is not in the plot but in the author's quest for truth, which has been Conrad's goal from the start of his writing career. "Truth alone is the justification of any fiction which makes the least claim to the quality of art." [3]

Conrad's object was to examine man's destiny, his weakness and strength, his goodness and evil. That and no less is the theme of *Victory,* of *Chance,* and of other novels and stories. The world, which treated Conrad and his family so cruelly, had little stability in Conrad's view. It is small wonder that this uprooted Pole regards the universe of nature and men with cautious aloofness which, however, never reaches Heyst's pessimism. In *A Personal Record,* a book written in an unusually sober mood, he notes that resignation is not indifference. He would not like to be a mere spectator on the bank of life. He would like to speak in a voice of sympathy and compassion. He advocates resignation, not mystic nor detached but open-eyed, conscious, and informed by love which is "the only one of our feelings for which it is impossible to become a sham." [4]

It is no use fighting against false fate, Conrad says through the narrator of the story "Falk." One does not quarrel with the elements. Falk has survived in a desperate struggle aboard an isolated ship, killing his opponent and eating his flesh. He is the epitome of human self-preservation, the preservation of the body and its senses. Falk has a most profound horror of death and will "guard his own life with *the inflexibility of a pitiless and immovable fate.*" [5]

Actually Falk is a symbol of this fate, of blind natural forces; therefore he must prevail.

Yet in most novels and stories of Conrad, death is not the most horrifying or pathetic thing, and he often dispatches his protagonists with a sense of philosophic resignation. Death does not always spell defeat. On the contrary, some of Conrad's works are concerned with man's victory over death and the blind forces of destiny. Death to an isolato is a welcome visitor, as Conrad learned in his childhood when he watched his father in the hours of disillusionment and gloom. From this experience as well as from Conrad's subsequent hardships and sufferings came the yearning for peace, which often took the form of the death-wish.

If we accept Mr. Baines's theory of Conrad's attempt upon his own life we add a new significance to Conrad's treatment of suicide; for it can now be related to his own self-destructive tendencies. But even if we assume that the duel between Conrad and Blunt did take place as described in *The Arrow of Gold*, Conrad's fiction indicates his preoccupation with suicide. This was evident already at the outset of his writing career. As he was struggling with his second novel, *An Outcast of the Islands*, Conrad wrote to Mme. Poradowska:

I have burnt nothing. One talks like that and then courage fails. *People talk this way of suicide!* And then something is always lacking: sometimes it is strength, sometimes perseverance, sometimes courage. The courage to succeed or the courage to recognize one's impotence. What remains always indelible and cruel is *the fear of finality.* One temporizes with fate, or tries to outwit desire, or attempts to juggle with his life. Men are always cowards. They are afraid of "nevermore." I believe that only women have true courage.[6]

If we do not agree with the Freudian critic that Conrad sublimated his own desire to commit suicide by making so many of his protagonists kill themselves, we must at least note Conrad's emphasis on death as deliverance and his insistence on self-sacrifice. He confesses that his dedication to the writing profession was a sacrifice of his own life. During his sea years he sometimes wished himself dead.

Marlow, who is often the spokesman for Conrad himself, hints that he, too, contemplated suicide at one time. But Marlow's death-wish is closer to that of Heyst, and, in a sense, identical with that of Lena. It is a wish which is inherent in the romantic self-sacrifice for the sake of an ideal or a loved person. This sacrifice is almost invariably futile, for it does not win the cause of the victim, nor save the victim himself, but opens to him a source of moral and spiritual redemption. The chivalrous struggle of a hero against overwhelming odds has always been a favorite subject with the romantic writers. English, French and German literatures boast an imposing gallery of characters who perish in a vain but gallant fight against unpropitious destiny, and so does Polish literature. Most of the great Polish romantic poets deal with this theme.

Conrad himself knew the meaning of the struggle for a lost cause. Writing to Cunninghame Graham in 1899 on the subject of social democratic tendencies among the Warsaw University youth, he found that nothing was permitted him except "a fidelity to a cause absolutely lost, to an idea without a future." [7] One year later, he restated this conviction in *Lord Jim*. Marlow tells us that a certain readiness to perish is not so very rare, but it is seldom that one finds men prepared to fight a losing battle to the last, or to struggle against the elements of the stupid and brutal mob. Such men are castaways and wanderers. They who strive against "unreasonable forces" know well the feeling of utter weariness and the longing for rest. Humanity can never understand their subtle search for the true essence of life.

What matters in Conrad's fiction is not the predominance of "bad men" and the failures and misfortunes of "good men," but this argument about the true essence of life, which emerges from their conflict. The Kurtzes, the Heysts and the Decouds must ask themselves whether they sinned against the basic feelings and elementary convictions which make life possible to the mass of mankind. Conrad offers his characters the choice of a way of living. Man's helplessness against the forces of destiny does not prevent him from making his own decision. This Faustian theme, Alice Raphael suggests in her book, *Goethe the Challenger*, appears throughout *Victory*.[8] Heyst is Conrad's Faust; Jones is a nineteenth-century version of Mephistopheles. His appearance astonishes Heyst as the mysterious appearance of the travelling scholar surprises Faust. (The sudden arrival of Brown in Patusan has the same effect on Jim.) Heyst does not accept Jones as his unknown self but he draws a comparison between himself and the bandit. Jones, of course, does not mince words. Like Brown, in *Lord Jim*, he repeatedly points out to Heyst their mutual characteristics, and slyly notes that his presence on the island is no more morally reprehensible than Heyst's. Brown also reminds Jim of his past and hints at the fact that only some sort of a crime could have brought him into the wilderness. Both bandits tell their victims the story of their lawless lives. Jones and Brown are social outcasts who have rebelled against society. In his dying speech Brown calls himself the Scourge of God, blindly believing in the righteousness of his will against all mankind. Jones assumes a similarly arrogant attitude, and he clearly defines his role in the drama which he is about to enact:

In one way I am—yet, *I am the world itself,* come to pay you a visit. In another sense *I am an outcast*—almost an outlaw. If you prefer a less materialistic view, *I am a sort of fate—the retribution that waits its time.*[9]

Conrad repeated this theme in similar terms when he

analyzed Decoud, the ". . . victim of the disillusioned weariness which is *the retribution meted out to intellectual audacity.*" [10]

Thus, Brown and Jones are not only "the other selves" of Jim and Heyst. They are also the symbols of "*the implacable destiny of which we are the victims—and the tools.*" [11] The premonitions of Lena come true. Fate has closed in to punish them for their sins. Heyst's feeling of guilt, like his suicide, is symbolic of his return to humanity, because only those who accept the moral tenets of a social group can experience this emotion. Faust repudiates life and thus shuts evil out of his consciousness. Eventually, he must learn, like the Nietzschean man, to accept his own ugliest self. Faust can redeem himself and win his freedom only at the cost of physical death and the liberating effect of self-imposed purgatorial suffering. Heyst, after shutting out the experiences of common men from his life, must learn the meaning of love and hope. His final redemption is attained in the purgatory of fire—the price he has to pay for his alienation from the human community. Heyst "couldn't stand his thoughts before her dead body—and fire purifies everything." [12]

Here, as in *Almayer's Folly*, Conrad uses the concept of the *Flammentod* which was employed by Goethe and by many Victorian writers concerned with the problem of conversion.[13] Not that Conrad attempted to preach this problem. But it is obvious that Heyst, Razumov, Captain Anthony, the Captain in *The Shadow Line* (to mention but a few) are literary studies in that popular Victorian subject: man's spiritual new-birth. Even Almayer, who cannot be reborn spiritually, tries to achieve a new identity by the symbolic burning of the house in which he has lived with his daughter. This fire, he vainly hopes, will destroy his old self, his great love for Nina.

Fire is not the only means by which to accomplish the purification of one's soul. Water, too, may be the agent of purification. Whether Conrad, like many Victorian writers, was aware of using baptismal symbolism is not known; his suicidal protagonists choose one of the two elements: fire or water. Thus, Captain Brierly, who resembles Heyst in being unable to stand his own thoughts, leaps overboard. Renouard's infatuation with Miss Moorsom drives him to suicide by drowning in the sea. Decoud shoots and drowns himself when he can no longer stand his loneliness.

In each of these cases there is a symbolic cleansing of the soiled self, a sort of expiation for a transgression. There is a discovery of the real self which man dare not face. Brierly cannot live with the consciousness of his cowardice. Renouard will not go on living with the memory of his unrequited love which has turned him into a liar and a weakling. His old personality disintegrates. His passion for Felicia is akin to Svidrigaïlov's love for Dunya in Dostoyevsky's *Crime and Punishment*. The affair ends with the suicide of the lover. Of course, it can be pointed out that unrequited fatal love is a favorite theme in nineteenth-century Polish literature (e.g., *The Doll* by B. Prus) or, for that matter, in the romantic literature that preceded it. What makes one compare Conrad's characters to those of Dostoyevsky is the morbid intensity of feeling displayed by the protagonists. Men like Svidrigaïlov, Renouard and Lingard (of *The Rescue*) stand on the verge of insanity. They cannot regain their old selves and, consequently, composure and confidence. The only way out of their moral dilemma is self-destruction.

Man does not know himself—that is the fundamental fact which Conrad's protagonists must learn, and often at the price of their own lives. The greatest danger is self-deception. Heyst's game is up because he has discovered this truth about himself: he cannot live without love, which means a firm tie with another human being, and a bond with all mankind. Decoud's isolation on the island has

shown him the unreality of his past existence. Winnie
Verloc's personality is torn into two parts, whose mental
operations do not adjust themselves very well to each
other. The loss of her idiot brother and her subsequent
murder of Mr. Verloc have revealed to her the mysterious
side of her nature. Alvan Hervey in the story "The Return"
finds out the shocking truth that his wife does not share
his opinion of himself and that there is an abyss between
them.

"The Return," an insignificant piece of work when compared to *Lord Jim* or *Nostromo,* is nevertheless an ironic
and fairly penetrating comment on man's vanity. The plot
of the story is very simple. Mrs. Hervey elopes with another
man, and suddenly comes back to her husband without
an explanation for her action. The moral stress caused by
her flight from home and her return brings finally the
knowledge to these two people that they have skimmed
over the surface of life, ignoring its dark, hidden stream.
The lone sermon on morality which Alvan Hervey de-
livers for the benefit of his mute and apparently non-
repenting mate, is a mere gesture to affirm something which
is no longer there. His moral precepts sound like plati-
tudes, and his admonitions to his wife to observe rigid
principles of respectability for the sake of respectability
are pompous and somewhat ludicrous. As he attempts to
find a logical explanation for the estrangement, his wife's
unfaithfulness assumes the proportions of a universal calamity. Actually, this estrangement has existed between
them all the time. During the five years of their marriage
the Herveys came to know each other sufficiently well for
all the purposes of their respectable existence, but they
were incapable of real intimacy. Mrs. Hervey has asserted
her individuality in a way which hurts a man's pride and
endangers the comfortable stolidity of his little world. He
has a holy terror of scandal. A scandal among the people
of his position, Alvan preaches dully, is disastrous for

morality. It is fatal for it aims against his loyalty—to the larger conditions of life. But Mrs. Hervey's return changes him radically. A new conscience is born of his pain. Morality, he now understands, is not a method of happiness but a terrible revelation.

His moral landmarks disappear one by one "consumed in the *fire of his experience,* buried in hot mud, in ashes." [14] He feels the destructive breath of passion. He has discovered the mysterious universe of moral suffering. All of a sudden Alvan Hervey stands nakedly alone. His own righteousness sweeps him away from the pinnacle of outraged dignity, and he loses his moral footing in the bitterness of his resentment against Mrs. Hervey. His solid universe has suddenly crumbled before the enigmatic attitude of an unfaithful wife. The world is no longer safe. Nothing could be foretold or guarded against. He has always believed that excess of feeling is unhealthy and morally unprofitable. Now, however, he is in a turbulent state of mind, and he experiences a sense of dangerous loneliness. His test is over when he perceives the barrenness of his old convictions and learns that there can be no life without faith and love, echoing Heyst's last utterance. Although Hervey does not leap into the flames, he contemplates a similar exit. "It was an awful sacrifice to cast all one's life *into the flame of a new belief.*" [15] He flees from his home because he cannot stand the uncertainty of the future without love and faith—a future which is doomed to be clouded with suspicion and hate.

As Alvan Hervey was misled by his greed for position, so Charles Gould was by his false faith in material interests. He is not corrupted by the symbolic silver mine in the sense that Nostromo is. With the Capataz de Cargadores, the silver is but an agent in his moral downfall. He steals it only after he discovers that four ingots of the treasure entrusted to him are missing. If he had known what happened to the missing ingots, it is very doubtful whether he would have committed the theft at all. He becomes a thief so that he might remain, in the eyes of the world, the symbol of incorruptibility. This is a constantly humiliating situation for him, because he cannot disclose to the world the source of his wealth and, moreover, he loses his former identity within the orbit of falsehood.

Charles Gould, on the other hand, is a victim of the mine which became to him the symbol of progress. His greed sets him apart from his wife and from the rest of the world. His passion for the silver mine is actually more than mere greed for the precious metal. It goes back to his father's failure to make the mine a prosperous enterprise. His struggle to succeed where his father failed, is an attempt to vindicate him morally. His sense of duty to himself and to the world becomes, as with the American millionaire Holroyd, a kind of religion. They are, in a sense, the missionaries of the San Tomé mine, their real church. It becomes to the Goulds a subject of rehabilitation and imposes upon them a moral obligation to be its slaves. But Gould's faith in the material interests is a breach of human solidarity.

Charles Gould's exalted devotion to his mine is sin. The penalty for it is alienation from his wife and ultimate destruction. Mrs. Gould saw clearly

. . . the San Tomé mine possessing, consuming, *burning up* the life of the last of the Costaguana Goulds; mastering the energetic spirit of the son as it had mastered the lamentable weakness of the father.[16]

Her own isolation is most pathetic, for she is immensely wealthy, respected, loved, yet one of the most solitary of Conrad's women. For her the victory of the last of the Goulds is indeed a terrible success. The silver mine is the symbol of the all-possessing corrupting power which sets men apart from ordinary human interests, and eventually destroys them. It ruins the lives of the guilty and the inno-

cent alike: Decoud, Nostromo, The Goulds, Dr. Monygham, Hirsch, Georgio, Viola, Linda, Giselle, Senor Avel-
lanos—in fact, almost all characters in *Nostromo* are its victims in one way or another. Man's fate is as mysterious
and sinister as the San Tomé mine. It is "like hate of invisible powers interpreted, made sensible and injurious by the
actions of men." [17] The invisibility of these powers makes
them incalculable. Devotion to one's duty, fidelity to one's
ideal—these are calculable things. Chance is not; it is irrational. To Conrad it represents a mighty force, irresistible
in its manifestations. Men's actions spring from the intentions for which they can be held responsible. "The ultimate effects of whatever they do are far beyond their
control." [18]

CHAPTER VI

THE EXPERTS IN THE PSYCHOLOGICAL WILDERNESS

CONRAD'S WORK cannot be studied without relating it to his own life, for a great deal of his writing is a dramatization of his own experiences and problems. The theme of betrayal and redemption, in particular, can be traced to his own feelings of insecurity and guilt. *The Shadow Line,* subtitled "A Confession," an intensely personal book, shows how well Conrad knew the meaning of moral anguish, and that he, too, had his "double." The description of Mills in *The Arrow of Gold* fits Conrad himself. Mills admits that he is a solitary man of books who has a secret taste for adventure. Although Conrad was most earnestly committed to order, self-control and fidelity to one's duty, he could not suppress his sympathy with the quixotic outcasts, the rogues, the men and women trapped by grim destiny.

The loneliness of the narrator in *The Shadow Line* is of the kind that plagued Lord Jim after his fatal jump from the *Patna.* It is the loneliness of a man assailed by the doubt of his own worth. The motto of the book, "worthy of my undying regard," chosen by Conrad from the text itself, is a revealing comment on his philosophy. Indeed, the things he regards most are the seamen's loyalty to their captain, and their ability to withstand the stress of adversity. The young man in command is horrified to learn of the immoral conduct of his predecessor who didn't care about his ship or the crew. Such behavior was *"a complete act of treason, the betrayal of a tradition* which seemed to [me] as imperative as any guide on earth could be." [1] This tradition, and the sense of continuity which it gives to men, holds Conrad's quixotic dreams in check and makes it possible for him to cherish life despite his gloomy view of man's strife. It is fitting that the seemingly unimaginative and moralizing Captain Giles in *The Shadow Line* expresses Conrad's philosophy best.

In the beginning of their acquaintance, the young narrator-captain resents Giles' benevolent air of wisdom. When he comes back from his severe trial at sea, convinced now that he has mastered not only the art of navigation but that he has overcome the weakness of his soul, he tells Giles the story of his hardships, listens to his sage and still irritating remarks and suddenly discovers he likes the old man and his solidity. Perhaps one of Giles' remarks has sunk into his mind: "A man should stand up to his bad luck, to his mistakes, to his conscience, and that sort of thing." [2]

It is hard to see how a man with Conrad's background can resemble the sedate and dull Captain Giles. The truth of the matter is that Giles's simple creed sums up Conrad's life as a faithful sailor and artist. As the latter, he has put a great deal of his personal experience into his fiction. The least veiled disguises of himself are his inimitable comentators on human destiny—the narrators of his novels and tales. They can afford the luxury of moralizing which he denies himself. Marlow is the most obvious other self of Conrad. In his early appearance he is a romantic baffled by the tragic aspects of reality. In *Chance*, written thirteen years after "Heart of Darkness," Marlow is no longer the hesitating, confused person. Ironic but still sympathetic, he has become an "expert in the psychological wilderness."[3] He has two worthy companions in D'Alcacer (*The Rescue*) and Stein (*Lord Jim*). All three are intellectual isolatoes who observe the universe with a skeptical melancholy and a philosophic indulgence for men's foibles.

In *Lord Jim* Marlow plays an intellectual Sancho Panza to Jim's Don Quixote. He has the same kind of imagination that makes Lord Jim an incurable romantic. He can therefore see Jim's point of view. Moreover, his probing into the meaning of Jim's conduct parallels the young man's craving for rehabilitation. Marlow will not stop until he has examined Jim's words and actions in every possible light. He wonders why he longed to go grubbing into the deplorable details of the *Patna* incident which, after all, concerned him "no more than as a member of an obscure body of men held together by *a community* of inglorious toil and by *fidelity to a certain standard of* conduct."[4] He replies to this question himself:

You may call it *an unhealthy curiosity*, if you like, but I have a distinct notion *I wished to find something*. Perhaps, unconsciously, I hoped I would find that something, some profound and *redeeming cause*, some merciful explanation, some convincing shadow of an excuse . . . Was it *for my own sake* that I wished to find some shadow of an excuse for that young fellow whom I had never seen before, but whose appearance alone added a touch of *personal concern* to the thoughts suggested by the knowledge of his weakness—made it *a thing of mystery* and terror. . . ?[5]

This, indeed, was the motive for his prying. Marlow was personally concerned with Jim because the knowledge of his weakness was like "a hint of *a destructive fate* ready for us all whose youth—in its day—had resembled his youth." [6] Marlow hoped to obtain some *exorcism* against the ghost of doubt. He was no mere bystander. The scrutiny of Jim's motives is an excuse for his own quest for his true identity. Marlow provides Conrad with the necessary perspective to analyze Jim's actions. Similarly, Stein and Brierly serve the same purpose in Marlow's psychological investigation.

Conrad's commentators seem to possess that foresight and that understanding of the protagonists' motives which is the creator's sole privilege. D'Alcacer, for instance, tells Lingard that Mrs. Travers will always remain in the fullest possession of herself. Lingard does not even listen to him. But D'Alcacer knows everything. He sums up the situation, he probes into Lingard's motives, for like a true Latin, he is not afraid of a little introspection. Since Lingard, Lord Jim or Captain Anthony are incapable of a philosophical analysis of their predicaments, Conrad provides them with those alert, interested and friendly observers who meditate aloud on their lot, drawing also on their own experiences. That is what makes them real characters and not merely Conrad's mouthpieces. "Whatever I have said," D'Alcacer says to Lingard (after his masterful description of *la femme fatale* as embodied by Mrs. Travers), "has come from my experience." Apologizing for his recollections, he claims to be quite out of his depth. That's how it should be. If he were not out of his depth, he would be in no position to regard Mrs. Travers and Lingard with that philosophic remoteness of his. He is like Conrad (and Marlow)—inside and outside of the book. When Mrs. Travers asks him a simple question: "Where has he gone?" (referring to Lingard), D'Alcacer replies with a symbol: "Where it's darkest, I should think." This sums up Lingard's position and the "moral" of the book. Only he and Conrad know that Lingard's infatuation with Mrs. Travers is bound to be fatal. For it is impossible to say how much complex *intuitive knowledge* was buried under his unruffled manner. This knowledge is admitted only to those who are like D'Alcacer, "detached in a sense from the life of men."[7] Therefore he is one of those men who are never completely in the dark in any given set of circumstances. D'Alcacer plays a role similar to that performed by Stein in *Lord Jim*. Both of them throw light on the mysteries of the hero's mind, and make conclusive remarks about the danger of the immersion in a dream.

Stein, who is solitary but not misanthropic (if he were that he would be denied contact with Marlow and Jim, and would thus be in no position to expound his views), is also a romantic dreamer. Yet he is a pessimist who knows that his ideals cannot be attained. With him, romanticism is not merely a personal necessity; it is "the heart pain—the world pain."[8] His very attachment to his world of butterflies shows that he views the world of men and women from a certain distance. He is not *of* the world.

D'Alcacer meditating on the dangers into which the folly of Lingard has exposed him, is similarly not concerned with human existence. He "attached no high value to life."[9] It can be seen, therefore, that D'Alcacer, Stein and Marlow, who are the confidants (or perhaps the confessors) of the unfortunate sinners against human solidarity, are guilty of the same transgression. They are not full citizens of the community of mankind.

CHAPTER VII

PURELY HUMAN

My point of view . . . is purely human . . .[1]

OUR WORLD HAS WITNESSED a spectacle of gigantic physical and moral destruction. We have not yet recovered from the horrors of World War II, and already we are faced with a prospect of even greater danger—that of atomic Armageddon. Facing the prospect of utter chaos and desolation we often feel lost and insecure. Much of Conrad's present revival and recognition is due, I think, to his preoccupation with the theme of isolation, which has a special significance in our modern world. Conrad's world of lonely captains and adventurous outcasts may seem remote to us; few modern writers need send their heroes to distant, exotic lands to dramatize their loneliness and spiritual conflicts. But Conrad's treatment of the isolated man brings him close to the contemporary writer, even though the modern critic will sometimes be tempted to regard Conrad as a belated and fuzzy romantic, whose themes of betrayal and expiation have been made relevant by the work of much more hard-headed novelists (and

politically better informed) than he was. It is obvious that
Conrad's reputation benefited from it, but it is doubtful
whether the intrinsic value of Conrad's art has anything to
do with the accuracy of his political or sociological views.
His strength often lies in the absence of abstruse issues
and the emphasis on those human emotions which are true
at all times.

Conrad, the romantic, has a great feeling for simple-
minded, primitive men and for nature. But his idealized
picture of the elemental is so tempered by his realistic
vision that a certain basic dichotomy is the result. Conrad
regards the primitives with a sympathetic yet analytic
curiosity, not unlike the enlightened tourist with a Baedeker
in his hand. He himself can never be *of* these people but he
can feel *for* them and identify himself with them. This he
does as a thinker contemplating mankind with an Olympian aloofness rather than as a romantic reformer carried
away by his own ardor.

Conrad's people are like Chekhov's—always becoming
infatuated with those who cannot requite their affections,
always dreaming of goals which are beyond their reach.
Like Chekhov, Conrad never moralizes, nor does he attempt
(as Dostoyevsky and Tolstoy do) to create a simple moral
order based on preconceived maxims. He writes of the
world as he sees it, discovering in it a few virtues that stand
out in the pathos of human weakness. The difference between the two is that Conrad's tales of failure are often
stories of heroism and spiritual triumph while Chekhov's
are mere glimpses into the nature of humanity, dramatic
epigrams on the nineteenth-century Russian society.

It is perhaps this strange blend of romanticism and
realism that accounts for Conrad's appeal to the modern
reader. His romantic egoists and social outcasts have many
counterparts in the novels of authors like D. H. Lawrence,
Virginia Woolf and James Joyce. Gerard Crich, Ursula
Brangwen, Gudrun and Loerke in D. H. Lawrence's *Women*

in Love, are enclosed within their own dreams, unable to get in touch with other human beings. Mrs. Ramsay's vision in *To the Lighthouse* and the lighthouse itself symbolize the contrast between real-life experience and the ideal truth which man is seeking—a typically Conradian subject. The romantic Septimus in *Mrs. Dalloway* becomes as disillusioned as young Marlow (and so many other characters of Conrad), who in different words said that it might be possible that the world itself is without meaning. And the feeling of loneliness and chaos evoked by Mr. Ramsay's habitual "we perished each alone" recalls Conrad's Heyst. Similarly, Gabriel and Gretta in James Joyce's "The Dead" are as shut-in as Charles Gould and his wife in *Nostromo.* Stephen (of *A Portrait of the Artist as a Young Man*) and Lord Jim share the "isolating" imagination, the sense of gnawing remorse and the morbid quest for self-revelation.

The literature of our times is largely concerned with estrangement and exile. Tonio Kröger's query, whether the artist is at all a man, has been asked by every major modern writer who has experienced a sense of "cosmic exile" or the tragic particularity of selfhood. It is a question Conrad must have asked himself many times as he "wrestled with the Lord" for his creation. For he could write only by means of descending to that lonely sphere of conflict within himself. He counselled the young writer to squeeze out of himself every sensation, thought and image and urged him to explore the darkest corner of his heart.

The isolated man is found in the literature of all periods. But it is the nineteenth century that particularly is concerned with the individual estranged from his group by his sensibility, by social ostracism or else by the inscrutable decrees of destiny. Thus, the romantic writer finds himself deprived of moral values and he revolts by stressing his individuality and by endowing Nature with what mechanized civilization lacks. He contemplates Nature in solitude; he stresses the theme of alienation. His loves are desperate

and fatal; his exploits dangerous and remote from the realities of this world which he detests and renounces. His
inspired idealism and his ardent faith in the possibility of
bettering the world turn him into a rebel against his own
society and an exile from it.

Conrad and some of his heroes share Byron's essential
duality. Byron, the man of action, is also the poet, morbidly
displaying his sense of guilt. Conrad, the successful and
resolute sea captain is also the aloof, agonized thinker and
artist. But Conrad does not rebel against mankind, and his
romantic isolatoes are not imitations of Byronic characters.
Byron and his heroes cherish the idea of the man who is
a law unto himself. While some Conradian protagonists
bear this peculiar imprint of romanticism, they differ in
persistently recognizing the existence of a certain code of
behavior. If or when they break it, they suffer the penalty
of isolation. The Byronic romantic needs no such code for
he is satisfied with his own world.

Conrad's treatment of the isolated man shows affinities
with the romantic as well as with the Victorian points of
view. His mistrust of reason, his profound realization of
mystery in man and nature, his glorification of personal
honor and the *Weltschmerz* are romantic traits that strike
at the very root of Victorian orthodoxy and complacency.
His respect for self-control and sanity, his awareness of
"this strange disease of modern life," are Victorian. Like
Matthew Arnold, he pictures himself wandering between
two worlds, one dead and the other powerless to be born.
He shares Arnold's vision of the dreamlike world without
joy, or love or light or certitude. He dislikes (consciously,
at any rate) extremes of emotions, for which he castigates
Dostoyevsky.

But Conrad, the sober critic, is not Conrad the story-
teller whose heroes do not lack excess of emotion, nor do
they retain self-control as fate closes in upon them. And
Conrad himself, it might be added, was not exactly a model

of calculated sobriety in his two lives as seaman and artist. He acted on impulse, lost his temper, indulged in violent likes and dislikes. It is characteristic that Conrad condemns and hates what he fears might be true of himself. His dream of a world governed by sanity evoked in him distaste for writers like Dostoyevsky (whose dislike of Poles was an additional spur to Conrad's feeling of revulsion). But the spirit of Dostoyevsky, more than that of any other writer, animates men like Razumov, Lord Jim, Verloc and the host of anarchists, criminals, would-be saints and all sorts of moral and social outcasts. And the morbidity of *The Secret Agent,* of *Lord Jim* and of so many other works, is the morbidity (as well as the fascination) of *The Idiot, Crime and Punishment* and *The Brothers Karamazov.* Conrad's men and women, like Dostoyevsky's, are uncommon people, often more than life-size. Their lives are concerned with matters of fidelity and betrayal, with problems of courage and compassion. And, for all their differences, both are moralists intensely preoccupied with human conduct.

In his anthology *Existentialism from Dostoyevsky to Sartre* Dr. Walter Kaufmann includes such different writers as Nietzsche, Dostoyevsky, Rilke, Kafka, Jaspers, Heidegger, Camus and Sartre, claiming for them one common feature—"their perfervid individualism."[2] Since Conrad, no less than Dostoyevsky or Sartre, manifests the quality of uncompromising individualism, we may inquire whether his view of the human condition is similar to that of the modern existentialist thinker. Jean-Paul Sartre, who has been largely responsible for the dramatization of extentialism in literature, shows some remarkable similarities with Conrad, as well as significant differences.

Sartre views man as a creature conceived for no specific purpose, his life subject to an indifferent fate, his freedom unlimited and therefore expressed in purely arbitrary preferences. Perhaps if all Sartre wanted to express were the pointlessness of man's existence, he would not be much different from a writer like Hardy, whose heroes face the unjust and senseless verdicts of destiny, and rebel against them. But Sartre (and Conrad) goes farther than merely expressing a protest against blind destiny. The core of his work is the preoccupation with man's commitment and decision, man's loneliness in the universe, man's contradictory nature. Man chooses himself by his commitment and thus becomes the sole arbiter of his freedom. Existence means freedom, but this freedom is that nothingness in man's heart, which compels the human reality to make itself, instead of being itself. This extreme vision of human freedom serves to emphasize the dominant themes of existentialism: the "either-or" quality of man's lot, the unpredictability of his life, his guilt and anxiety feelings and his final limit of death. The full realization of man's mortality forces man to make the choice of his life, which is an authentic choice *because* it is made face to face with death.

In *Nausea* (first published in 1938) Sartre tells the story of Antoine Roquentin, a French writer who keeps a brutally frank diary. This hero is possessed by an overwhelming sensation of nausea which he experiences both in himself and in the outer world.

So this is Nausea: this blinding evidence? I have scratched my head over it! I've written about it. Now I know: I exist—the world exists—and I know that the world exists. That's all. It makes no difference to me. It's strange that everything makes so little difference to me: it frightens me.[3]

It is clear that this "nausea" has a symbolic value and that it is intended not only to express Roquentin's and Sartre's disgust with reality but also Sartre's vision of the world's absurdity. This conception of the alienation of the world is perhaps the main tenet of existentialism.

Conrad too was aware of the absurdity and the inscrutability of nature and the human condition. As early as in 1898 he professed his belief to Cunninghame Graham that

. . . there is no morality, no knowledge, and no hope; there is only the consciousness of ourselves which drives us about a world . . . that is always but a vain and floating appearance.[4]

He did not think it was worth troubling about the fate of humanity condemned ultimately to perish from cold. He favored the attitude of "cold unconcern" as the only reasonable approach to life, suspecting that perhaps our appointed task on this earth was indeed only "the unwearied self-forgetful attention to every phase of the living universe reflected in our consciousness."[5] Conrad is resigned, for he has no faith with which to counteract his skeptical view of mankind's progress. Life, he tells us in his novels and stories, is a fascinating spectacle despite its horrors and tragedies; sometimes because of them. It most assuredly merits the artist's effort to record his impressions.

Both Conrad and Sartre knew great unhappiness in their youth. Conrad grew up in the atmosphere of national defeat and frustration that followed the ill-omened Polish insurrection of 1863. A son of exiles, soon an orphan and émigré, Conrad knew the meaning of death and defeat. Sartre matured in the pre-war France, torn by inner dissension and strife. He too learned the meaning of defeat under German occupation and came to the paradoxical conclusion that his fellow countrymen had first to be crushed before they understood the meaning of liberty.

In such works as *Nausea* or the play *The Flies* Sartre ridicules mankind and humanism; Conrad's works, while also revealing the lack of ethical aim in the world and the anguish of living, are often a limpid exposition of good and evil. The distinction between the two is made clear by the personal code of decency and faithfulness of the heroes. Sartre's characters do not have any code of behavior except in the sense of an unpredictable commitment they make in a moment of desperation or crisis.

Conrad the philosopher or, more accurately, Conrad the

letter-writer, may censure mankind severely and condemn its morals and its religions. Conrad, the novelist, creates unhappy, persecuted and lonely figures, driven to self-destruction and struck down by forces beyond their control. But these characters are not necessarily depressing or disgusting as are those of Sartre. In many instances, their destiny is tragic because they have the making of great men and their own shortcomings as well as chance bring about their downfall; moreover, the self-sacrifice of Conrad's suffering man frequently has a purifying effect upon him and it reveals to him the ideal conception of his own personality—the essence of his existence as a human being. For example, Lord Jim and Razumov have no true knowledge of themselves. When they discover their own cowardice (in a truly Sartrean preoccupation with the subject), they seek death as a solution to their problems, as a means of moral redemption and perhaps also as a means of self-assertion— their final act of free will.

When Sartre deals with a similar problem he does not recognize the morality of liberation and salvation, for his "free" individuals are forever in a state of conflict with other men. In *Existentialism and Humanism*[6] Sartre considers *his* view of human existence as optimistic because it gives man a chance to shape his own destiny. "There is no other universe," Sartre avers, "except the human universe, the universe of human subjectivity."[7] And it is the eternal presence of man, not within himself but in a human universe, that Sartre calls existential humanism. It is the relation of man's transcendence to subjectivity. Man is his sole legislator and he alone must make his decisions.

The treatment of love and sex by these two writers again presents similarities and differences. Both Conrad and Sartre show the fundamental loneliness and apartness of man from woman, even in situations commonly considered to be intimate. But Conrad's lovers are romantic and rather chivalrous souls, often torn by a conflict between their passion and their sense of honor. Love to Conrad is either a brusque or chivalrous tenderness of man toward woman and the passive submission of the latter; or else it is a consuming passion which is as paralyzing to the hero as the self-probing restlessness of a Jim. Men and women fall under the spell of its illusion only to find the dream turn into a nightmare. The romantic dream and the realistic nightmare are both characterized by man's inherent separateness.

Love and sex mean something totally different to Sartre. He is openly cynical in his attitude toward the former. There can be no true love where the relationship of one individual toward another is based only on conflict and dominance. In Sartre's works sex is blatant, aggressive and usually associated with physical filth and images suggesting revulsion. Where Conrad speaks of the tragedy of noble souls that cannot come to terms with the harsh realities of life, Sartre paints scenes of amorality and vacuousness, shocking to the squeamish mind.

In the story "Intimacy" the relationship between Lulu and Henri is anything but a romantic picture of marital bliss; the title is ironic, for theirs is a brutal and heartless sort of intimacy. Henri and Lulu sleep naked in the same bed and are shown in some of the more sordid physical aspects of their domesticity (soiled underwear and *urinoirs* seem to be especially fascinating to Sartre). What links them together is not love but an abject, slavish and maso-chistic submission on Henri's part and a somewhat sadistic and cynical affection of Lulu for her husband. Conventional morality simply does not exist for these people. Yet it is to Sartre's credit that he makes his characters come alive and their vices not quite wicked.

In "Erostratus" Sartre gives an almost clinical, yet fictionally successful, analysis of a sexual deviate and criminal. Erostratus (Paul Hilbert) is but a poor shadow of Dostoyevsky's Raskolnikov and his dream of power. The dominant emotion is again a kind of nausea—a profound disgust Paul

Hilbert has for *other* men. It is little wonder that, after shooting his victim, he winds up in a public lavatory with one bullet left in his revolver, which he has kept for himself. At the last moment, however, he does not have the courage to shoot himself, and he throws away his revolver, opening the door through which his captors will reach him. He has made his decision.

As an uncompromising atheist Sartre denies the existence of God; faith in God is a myth which gives men a false feeling of security and prevents them from assuming the full, anguished responsibility of making their own choice. Man's freedom, therefore, means freedom from any illusory myth, freedom to make his own world. By the negation of all the myths (and this could mean men's past civilization) and by the realization of nothingness a person can achieve the state of absolute freedom.

Conrad resembles both Sartre and Dostoyevsky in depicting lives that are full of melodramatic fury and shocking violences. But where Sartre quarrels with the established human institutions, Dostoyevsky and Conrad are more concerned with the duality of the human soul and the struggle within it. Yet Conrad differs from Sartre and Dostoyevsky, for he does not expound the gospel of Christianity nor atheistic theories. None of his several versions of a Don Quixote is as Christ-like as Myshkin, but each is as detached from the circumstances of ordinary life as Dostoyevsky's saintly but often ridiculous figure. Heyst, Jim and Lingard have no religion. What makes them resemble Don Quixote and Myshkin is the conclusion that may be drawn from their lives—that man's agony and loneliness are futile, yet worth telling.

Dostoyevsky always seeks for God and man's salvation through God. In Conrad's work there is no such search. Conrad finds Christianity distasteful and irritating although he acknowledges it is "great, improving, softening, compassionate." He resents its "impossible standards and the anguish it has brought to innumerable souls—on this earth." [8]

One need not suppose that such irascible comment is close to Sartre's militant atheism; indeed, nothing could be more misleading. If anything, Conrad's protagonists evince all the good qualities of an "improving, softening, compassionate" faith even when there is no adherence to formal religion among them. What Conrad preaches, if he can be said to preach at all, is the gospel of individuality. However, while man must retain his own self, from which he cannot escape, he should not forget the ties that bind him to the human community. This is the moral law that can be deduced from all of his writings. The Fichthean dictum, "Act according to thy own conviction of duty," expresses Conrad's beliefs. An erroneous conviction of man's duty, which opposes the principle of Human Solidarity, is always punished. Those Conradian individualists who smack of the Nietzschean superman suffer the fate Melville assigned to Ahab—that is, total defeat.

Conrad also distinguishes the two central themes of freedom and negation. But the metaphysical and moral conclusions that can be deduced from the behavior of his heroes are quite different from those of Sartre. It is true that men like Decoud (in *Nostromo*) commit suicide when faced with the crushing state of loneliness and nothingness. In Sartre the universe is metaphysically void and therefore confrontation with emptiness does not have a destructive influence upon the hero: in Conrad, on the other hand, the sudden awareness of such metaphysical emptiness is fatal. Moreover, it is by dint of a positive identification with some ethical code of behavior that the Conradian hero achieves his personal freedom of choice and thereby his moral redemption.

Perhaps the main distinction between the Sartrean hero (e.g., Orestes in *The Flies*, who sets himself free from his final myth) and the Conradian protagonist, lies in the fact that the former becomes himself only when he recognizes the nothingness, the pointlessness of the world—when he can make the authentic choice in terms "Rather death than. . . ." Thus, Orestes can receive no help from supernatural sources and he himself must assume the guilt when he appears before Jupiter who serves as a kind of a cosmic Gestapo chief.

In Conrad's fiction, the unreflecting hero has no trouble at all in making the right decision; those who think too much and have no attachment to society or some ideal succumb to the forces of nature or to evil without struggle or escape from life by self-destruction. Others find their true selves *precisely* at the moment of the *right* decision, the moral decision of their lives, which sets them free in the sense that they as individuals are permitted to respond to their personal concept of fidelity. Even in the extreme case of a man like Heyst, whose egoism and philosophic alienation from the world are his and Lena's undoing, we have the moment of redemption, implied perhaps by the title. Of course, one may view such redemption as essentially ironic, since their mutual self-sacrifice appears to be a confirmation of the tragic senselessness of man's destiny.

Conrad's characters are not happy people, but the state of happiness is not excluded from their lives as an impossibility. Indeed, sometimes they achieve a state of exalted happiness at the moment of supreme self-sacrifice (e.g., Lord Jim). Sartre's view of man's birth as a wrong that cannot be righted eliminates happiness. What brings Sartre and Conrad together is their interest in man's morality. Sartre's attitude is one of absolutism. His heroes are cast into desperate situations and are left to themselves, to make use of their freedom to act as individuals, to make the all-or-nothing decision of their lives. Man's situation, as Sartre studies it, is meaningless, but occasionally his protagonists act as idealistically as those of Conrad although their affirmation seems perhaps sullied by his "nauseated" view of humanity. Thus, in his story, "The Wall" the anonymous

hero goes through the tortures of waiting for his own execution; when he finally makes his choice for the positive freedom of self-sacrifice, he does not seem to understand the
reasons for his courage. He does not like Ramon Gris, but
he would rather die than betray him. The act of courage
is performed almost nonchalantly. The hero is amused by
the insignificance of it all.

Undoubtedly I thought highly of him: he was tough. But this
was not the reason that I consented to die in his place; his life
had no more value than mine; no life had value. . . . I thought
to hell with Spain and anarchy; nothing was important. Yet I
was there, I could save my skin and give up Gris and I refused
to do it. I found that somehow comic; it was obstinacy. I
thought, "I must be stubborn!" and a droll sort of gaiety spread
over me.[9]

When the *falangistas* come for an answer he tells them that
Gris is hiding in the vault of a cemetery—a piece of information he believes to be a lie but which, by uncanny (or shall
we say cynical) coincidence, proves to be true.

It is interesting to note that at this moment of his courage the man feels stunned and malicious rather than proud;
and he regards this heroic part of himself as belonging to
someone else.

. . . this prisoner obstinately playing the hero, these grim
falangistas with their moustaches and their men in uniform running among the graves; it was irresistibly funny.[10]

His reaction upon learning the truth about the capture of
Gris is a state approaching hysteria; he laughs so hard
that he cries. Sartre has made his point: life is absurd,
incongruous. Still, we are left with the impression of a
courageous man; also with the impression that Sartre tends
to be cynical where Conrad is merely ironic or detached.
Yet neither this story nor the play *No Exit* (which

also deals with the problem of collaboration with the enemy) shows an intrinsic interest in the problem itself. Sartre does not delve into the deeper moral issues of betrayal and redemption that preoccupy Conrad in so many of his works. The sole moral issue here seems to be that of the hero's personal character or, more precisely, the issue whether or not he is a coward. Sartre will admit no heroic dimension in man, which is consistent with his theory of existentialism. Not for Sartre's heroes the "eternal constancy" or the "shadowy ideals of conduct" of a Jim; nor the inner moral conflict which plagues numerous Conradian characters. Only a few of Conrad's heroes are of the anti-hero type, while most of Sartrean protagonists belong in this category. The Conradian hero also fails in his self-sacrifice, but at least he has undergone a moral purgation or he has made a case for an affirmative attitude toward life by drawing a clear distinction between good and evil. When his world is absurd it is, like Kafka's, ironically absurd.

The world of Sartre is ugly, sickening and nightmarish. One cannot upbraid him, for the reality of France as he knew it before and during the war was not pretty. But it is one thing to observe evil, filth and chaos; it is another to see nothing else. Sartre's view of life as a vast nastiness and absurd existence is too one-sided to be universally true. Conrad's vision of the world is more rewarding aesthetically as well as morally. He too has lost his illusions, but not a sense of human values. Sartre reveals the incongruous and the pathological in man; Conrad his moral complexity. Conrad's world is as sad as that of Sartre, but only the latter is depressing in the final count. Sartre seems to be rationalizing on the theme of resistance to evil, and occasionally his analysis of the relationship of the evil-doer and his victim is brilliant. Rarely does he present Conrad's timeless issues of man's success and failure, of his terrible loneliness when he plunges into a moral conflict with himself.

To sum up the differences between the two writers:

Sartre's characters cannot attain to tragedy for, by definition, they exist in a metaphysical emptiness; Conrad's heroes may suffer as much as Sartre's do—they almost invariably meet with a violent death or languish in solitude—but even in their extreme state of isolation or defeat they are an affirmation of human fidelity and compassion. Their destiny can arouse in the reader the feelings of catharsis, without which there can be no perception of tragedy; Sartre's cannot, for his view of the universe of man and nature as absurd excludes the possibility of tragedy, which presupposes the existence of some ethical pattern of behavior. In Conrad we find the self-conscious and often moralizing Marlow (serving as a foil to Kurtz), the romantic dreamers like Lord Jim, Lingard, Stein and the stern men of the sea, dedicated to their ideals of service. Conrad's vision is not one of stark tragedy alone, but Sartre's is almost always a view of implacable darkness from which no one is permitted to withdraw, where men have nearly lost their humanity.

Sartre is not merely a writer of fiction. He is also a philosopher and a satirist. His essays and his fiction clearly reflect his political attitude. His political preferences, those of the extreme Left, are seen in the characterization of his heroes and in the treatment of his subjects. The intellectual analysis of a political problem and the solution to this problem are often more important than the essentially fictional aspects of his narrative. Sartre is committed to politics both in life and in his writings. Conrad's temperament, on the other hand, was hostile to politics. But, paradoxically, he turned to the world of anarchists, revolutionaries and émigrés in *Under Western Eyes, The Secret Agent* and *Nostromo.*

In his book, *Politics and the Novel,*[11] Mr. Irving Howe discusses Conrad as a political novelist. His essay offers some brilliant ideas about Conrad's treatment of politics. For instance, he speaks of two Conrads, one Jamesian who

directs, the other Dostoyevskian who erupts. He shows the
political strengths and weaknesses of Conrad's novels and
his astonishing, often prophetic insight into the life of politics. Yet Mr. Howe notes that Conrad eventually strives for
a non-political resolution of his political themes, thus admitting that Conrad may not be a political novelist in the
first place. Other writers considered in his book are certainly more aptly chosen for his particular scrutiny, e.g.,
Ignazio Silone, Arthur Koestler, George Orwell, Dostoyevsky—who can legitimately be considered as political novelists.

Dostoyevsky, while not a political novelist *par excellence,* was preoccupied with ideas. But Dostoyevsky's creative process was from an idea (religious, moral or political)
towards the building of a character. Being a great artist,
he succeeded in dramatizing his heroes so well that each of
them is a personality in his own right. This is what Conrad did too, but his method was to proceed from a particular man towards an idea which was rarely developed into
a consistent philosophy. It was, moreover, a wholly intuitive approach, like that of Meredith. Conrad was fascinated
by the individual personality of man—not by his political
and social conditions as such.

Conrad's approach to politics has more in common with
Henry James than with Dostoyevsky. *The Princess Casa-
massima* and such books of Conrad as *The Secret Agent*
and *Under Western Eyes,* may be considered as studies in
the temper of anarchism. But the radical creed itself is not
important except as the chief motivating force acting upon
the characters. The politics of these novels are merely a
framework within which Conrad lays bare the souls of his
protagonists. Of course, Conrad held certain political views
but, essentially, he is not a political novelist, for the latter
is *primarily* interested in political ideas.

Modern political novelists like Arthur Koestler, André
Malraux and Ignazio Silone view the problem of isolation

in terms of class conflict and the struggle between democracy and totalitarianism. Conrad, on the other hand, is closer to writers like James Joyce, Virginia Woolf, D. H. Lawrence and William Faulkner, who deal with the alienation of the individual. The political novelist approaches a problem from the abstract. Ideas and conflicts between two parties are more important to him than his characters' private lives. The protagonists of Arthur Koestler, for example, are mostly puppets who harangue the reader from their sundry soap-boxes. If they are interesting, it is mainly because their talk is stimulating, not because they are portrayed as living human beings. Without Koestler's basic political thesis Rubashov loses the illusion of reality. The novelist has not achieved the fusion between the personal and the political elements of his story. In contrast, such novels as Silone's *Fontamara, Bread and Wine*, Malraux's *Man's Fate* are successful both as novels and as political debates.

The literary quality of Conrad's works has little or nothing to do with the political aspects of some of his novels. Those of his characters who have a political identity should not be considered apart from his other protagonists who seem to exist outside of the realm of politics. The chief problem in *Under Western Eyes* is not anarchism and Conrad's treatment of the Russians, but Razumov and his moral struggle. Similarly, the fall of the Verlocs in *The Secret Agent* is a psychological not a political issue. In *Nostromo*, where Conrad created a whole republic, thus also giving a detailed account of Costaguana's politics, it was not his aim to grapple with tangible contemporary problems. Conrad's predominant interest was in the spiritual and moral plight of his protagonists. Admittedly, it would have been impossible to depict the disintegration of Decoud's will to live without the picture of Costaguana's internal strife; nor could the estrangement between Charles Gould and his wife be so well presented without the background of the

San Tomé mine and its role in the politics of the country. The question is what comes first—the characters or the political struggle in which they are involved. It seems to me that in Conrad's creative method the characters come first.

They are not illustrations of his political or social theories. Conrad is interested less in their ideas than in their temperaments. He views their fate with the eyes of a confirmed pessimist. Like Thomas Hardy, he shows his heroes facing the unjust and senseless verdicts of destiny. But where Hardy rebels and protests, Conrad merely exposes them to the reader, often with an ironic twinkle in his eyes. He shows evil in the life of men because he cannot help seeing it, and seeing is the primary duty of the novelist. Conrad goes beyond Hardy in that he is determined to analyze the causes of evil, even when it is clear that nothing can be done to stop it. He transcends the simplicity of Hardy's tragedy and he reveals the tortured conscience of the modern.

His closest psychological counterparts are such writers as William Faulkner, F. Scott Fitzgerald and Graham Greene, whom Albert J. Guerard discusses in his excellent book *Conrad the Novelist*. Conrad also invites comparison with several contemporary French novelists. Albert Camus's *The Stranger*, for example, explores some typically Conradian aspects of isolation. The inexorability of Meursault's fate, his interminable argument with himself and his awareness of solitude—all these remind us of the predicament of Lord Jim and Razumov. Similarly, Kyo's moral choice in André Malraux's *Man's Fate* is akin to Jim's and Razumov's moral resolution to sacrifice themselves. Malraux shares Conrad's tragic view of human fate and his heroes' apartness. François Mauriac, despite his Catholicism and moralistic attitude, also resembles Conrad, for his major theme is incommunicability, human loneliness. *The Desert of Love*, by his own admission, would be a good title for his entire work. Like Conrad, Mauriac reveals man's destiny and his true moral nature in a moment of crisis, usually fatal. He also dramatizes the incommunicability of people and their immobilization by their own passions.

In revealing the complexities of man's spiritual isolation Conrad went farther than his contemporaries. Wells and Galsworthy, to mention but two writers with whom he maintained close connections, belong to their particular period. Conrad's castaways and pariahs look forward to the twentieth century which produces its own typical isolato, marked by a guilt-ridden conscience. Psychoanalysis has made the novelist increasingly aware of the problem of guilt and expiation. Modern man lacks stability in a society that encroaches upon the freedom of the individual more than before. The prevalent "join-the-movement" creed, the drive toward conformity caused by the widespread mechanization of our lives, the lack of personal standards resulting in group-psychology—these forces are responsible for *other-directed* people who are solitary members of the lonely crowd because they can never come close to others; but the *inner-directed* man, whose character and conformity are insured by his early acquisition of an internalized set of goals, as well as the *tradition-directed* man are also members of the lonely crowd.[12]

The isolated men of Conrad belong, with a multitude of variations, to one of these three major types. It is not difficult to classify them into psychological, philosophical or literary categories. It is impossible, however, to classify Conrad the writer. He is a romantic, yet his romanticism is not quite English nor wholly Polish. He is a realist and yet he does not rely on the customary devices of the literary realists. He is an impressionist, yet his impressionism is but one of the many aspects of his art of fiction. Many of his works are peopled by sailors, but he is no mere spinner of romantic sea-yarns. And although some of his books deal with politics, he is not a political novelist.

The more one reads Conrad, the more one comes to realize that he belongs to no school. His personality as well as his work defy dogma. His achievements, he would have us believe, are simply due to the fact that he "followed [my] instinct: the voice from inside." [13] He modestly saw himself as "just another individual somewhat out of the common." [14] This the numerous lovers of Conrad will dismiss as an understatement. Even the average reader can see in him a very extraordinary figure. The discerning student, however, will regard his best novels and tales as the work of a great tragic writer.

A CHRONOLOGICAL LIST
OF CONRAD'S WORKS

1895 *Almayer's Folly.*
1896 *An Outcast of the Islands.*
1896 *The Sisters* (unfinished; published in 1928).
1897 *The Nigger of the Narcissus.*
1898 *Tales of Unrest.*
   "The Idiots" (1896), "Karain" (1897), "The Lagoon" (1897), "An Outpost of Progress" (1897), "The Return" (1898).
1900 *Lord Jim.*
1902 *Youth, and Two Other Stories.*
   "Youth" (1898), "Heart of Darkness" (1898), "The End of the Tether" (1902).
1902 *Typhoon.*
1903 *Typhoon, and Other Stories.*
   "Amy Foster" (1901), "Tomorrow" (1902), "Falk" (1903).
1904 *Nostromo.*
1906 *The Mirror of the Sea.*
1907 *The Secret Agent.*
1908 *A Set of Six.*
   "An Anarchist" (1906), "The Brute" (1906), "Gaspar Ruiz" (1906), "The Informer" (1906), "The Duel" (1908), "Il Conde" (1908).
1911 *Under Western Eyes.*
1912 *A Personal Record.*
1912 *'Twixt Land and Sea.*
   "The Secret Sharer" (1910), "A Smile of Fortune" (1911), "Freya of the Seven Isles" (1912).

1912 *Chance.*
1915 *Victory.*
1915 *Within the Tides*
"The Partner" (1911), "The Inn of the Two Witches" (1913), "Because of the Dollars" (1914), "The Planter of Malata" (1914).
1917 *The Shadow-Line.*
1919 *The Arrow of Gold.*
1920 *The Rescue* (begun 1896).
1921 *Notes on Life and Letters* (Reprints).
1923 *The Rover.*
1925 *Tales of Hearsay.*
"The Black Mate" (1908), "Prince Roman" (1911), "The Tale" (1917), "The Warrior's Soul" (1917).
1925 *Suspense* (unfinished).
1926 *Last Essays* (Reprints).

IN COLLABORATION WITH FORD MADOX FORD (HUEFFER)

1901 *The Inheritors.*
1903 *Romance.*
1924 *The Nature of a Crime.*

NOTES

Unless otherwise stated, the page numbers referring to the novels and stories of Joseph Conrad are those of the Edition of the Complete Works, Garden City, New York, Doubleday, Page & Co., 1924.

MOTTO AND INTRODUCTION

1. Antoni Lange (1862-1929), poet of the "Young Poland" movement. The stanza is taken from his poem "Solitude," quoted in Manfred Kridl's *Literatura Polska* (New York, 1945), p. 447. My translation.

2. Herman Melville, *Moby Dick* (London, 1922-24), I, p. 149. There is no evidence that Conrad was familiar with Melville's work.

CHAPTER I

THE INCORRIGIBLE DON QUIXOTE

1. *A Personal Record*, p. 110.

2. *The Portable Conrad*, "Prince Roman," New York, 1947, p. 58.

3. *Notes on Life and Letters*, "Poland Revisited," p. 169.

4. *Ibid.*, p. 171.

5. *A Personal Record*, "A Familiar Preface," p. xxi.

6. *Notes on Life and Letters*, "Poland Revisited," p. 168. Conrad's own reading list can be found in *A Personal Record*, pp. 70-72. A detailed list, based on Conrad's statements and the memoirs of F. M. Ford, G. Jean-Aubry and Galsworthy, has been compiled by M. R. Mélisson-Dubreil in her book, *La Personnalité de Joseph Conrad* (Paris, 1943), pp. 385-386.

7. *A Personal Record*, p. 124.

8. *Ibid.*, p. 44.

9. *Ibid.*, pp. 35-36.

10. *The Mirror of the Sea*, "Author's Note," p. viii.

11. *Ibid.*, My italics.

12. *Ibid.*, pp. 141-142. My italics. "The accuracy of the facts related in *The Mirror*," Aubry writes, "cannot be doubted." G. Jean-Aubry, *Joseph Conrad: Life and Letters* (2 vols., New York, 1927), I, 41. Hereafter cited as *Life and Letters*. Mr. Albert J. Guerard explains that neither the "G" nor the "Georges" nor the "Gérard" used with the name Jean-Aubry is correct. The actual name of the author was Jean Aubry. See Guerard's *Conrad the Novelist* (Cambridge, 1958), p. 307.

13. Letter to J. C. Squire, August 21, 1919. Quoted by Gérard Jean-Aubry, *The Sea Dreamer* (New York, 1957), p. 71. My italics.

14. *The Arrow of Gold*, p. 256. My italics.

15. Gérard Jean-Aubry, *The Sea Dreamer*, p. 73.

16. Jocelyn Baines, *Joseph Conrad: A Critical Biography*, (New York, London, Toronto, 1960).

17. *Ibid.*, p. 53, note.

18. *Ibid.*,

19. Jerry Allen, *The Thunder and the Sunshine, A Biography of Joseph Conrad* (New York, 1958), pp. 164-165. My italics.

20. *Ibid.*, pp. 165-166.

21. Jocelyn Baines, *op. cit.*, pp. 53-54.

22. *Ibid.*, p. 447.

23. Before his death in 1926, Miss Allen tells us, Count de Melgar wrote his memoirs, which were edited and published by his son, Count Francisco de Melgar; el Conde de Melgar, *Veinte años con Don Carlos, Memorias de su Secretario el Conde de Melgar* (Madrid, 1940).

24. Jerry Allen, *op. cit.*, p. 123.

25. Jocelyn Baines, *op. cit.*, p. 57.

26. *The Arrow of Gold*, p. 351.

27. "The Laugh," first manuscript draft of *The Arrow of Gold*. *T. J. Wise Collection*, now in the British Museum, London. This passage is quoted in Jean-Aubry's *Sea Dreamer*, Appendix, pp. 287-288. My italics.

28. *Notes on Life and Letters*, pp. 150-151. My italics.

29. *Letters of Joseph Conrad, to Marguerite Poradowska, 1890-1920* (New Haven, London, 1940), pp. 38-39.

30. The Polish novelist Joseph Korzeniowski (1797-1863) is not related to Conrad.

31. Quoted by Ludwik Krzyzanowski, "Joseph Conrad: Some Polish Documents," *The Polish Review*, Vol. III, No. 1-2 (Winter-Spring, 1958), pp. 60-61. My italics except the French words.

32. Joseph Ujejski, *O Konradzie Korzeniowskim* (About Conrad Korzeniowski, Warsaw, 1936), p. 18.

33. *Ibid.*, p. 28.

34. The visit was described in *Tygodnik Wilenski* (The Wilno Weekly Magazine) No. 1 (1925), under the title "Odwiedziny u Conrada" (A Visit with Conrad). Quoted by L. Krzyzanowski, "Some Polish Documents," p. 60.

35. Quoted by Maria Dabrowska, *Szkice o Conradzie* (Sketches about Conrad), Panstwowy Instytut Wydawniczy (State Publishing Institute, Warsaw, 1959), Preface, p. 8. My translation.

36. *Letters from Conrad, 1895-1924*, Edited with Introduction and Notes by Edward Garnett (London, 1928), Introduction, p. x.

37. Ludwik Krzyzanowski, "Joseph Conrad's 'Prince Roman,'" *The Polish Review*, Vol. I, No. 4 (Autumn, 1956).

38. My translation. This collection appeared in an edition of 250,000 copies, published by *Gosudarstvennove Izdatelstvo Khudozhestvennoy Literatury* (State Publication of Belles-lettres, Moscow, 1959), edited by Yevgeny Lann; drawings by the artist Yevgeny Kogan.

39. S. Helsztynski, "Joseph Conrad—Czlowiek i Tworca" (Joseph Conrad—The Man and the Creative Writer), *Kwartalnik Neofilologiczny* (Neophilological Quarterly), published by the Polish Academy of Sciences, Neophilological Committee, 5th year, Number 1-2 (Warsaw, 1958), p. 49.

40. *A Personal Record*, A Familiar Preface, p. xxi.

41. Roza Jablkowska, "Z angielskich i amerykanskich studiow nad Conradem" (From English and American Studies of Conrad), *Neophilological Quarterly*, p. 112.

42. L. Krzyzanowski, "Some Polish Documents."

43. *A Personal Record*, pp. 44-45.

44. "Rozmowa z J. Conradem" (A Talk with J. Conrad); interview printed in *Tygodnik Illustrowany* (Illustrated Weekly Magazine, No. 16, 1914); quoted by Maria Dabrowska in *Sketches about Conrad*, p. 22. My translation.

45. *Conrad zywy* (The Living Conrad, London, 1957). A volume of essays on Conrad, published by the efforts of the Union of Polish Writers Abroad.

46. Maria Dabrowska, *Sketches about Conrad*.

47. For further discussion of this subject see below, Chapter Four, The Anatomy of Betrayal.

48. *The Living Conrad* was edited by Wit Tarnawski, chairman of the Polish Conrad Club in England.

49. Gustav Morf, *The Polish Heritage of Joseph Conrad* (London, 1930).

50. *Conrad to a Friend—150 Selected Letters from Conrad,*

edited by Richard Curle, (Garden City, New York, 1928), p. 147. My italics.

51. *The Nigger of the Narcissus.* To my Readers in America, p. ix.

52. *A Personal Record,* "A Familiar Preface," p. xv. Also:

> . . . every novel contains an element of autobiography— and this cannot be denied, since the creator can only express himself in his creation . . .

Ibid., pp. xvii-xviii. Also: "A writer of imaginative prose . . . stands confessed in his work." *Ibid.,* p. 95.

53. *Lord Jim,* p. 180.

54. *Life and Letters,* I, 195.

55. Quoted by Mélisson-Dubreil, *La Personnalité de Joseph Conrad,* p. 189.

CHAPTER II

TO FOLLOW THE DREAM

1. "Heart of Darkness," p. 158-159.

2. *Ibid.,* p. 126.

3. *The Rescue,* p. 74. My italics.

4. Letter to S. L. Sanderson, October 12, 1899. *The Portable Conrad* (New York, 1950), p. 735. My italics. The dream, of course, need not be of the romantic kind. The dream evoked by human greed (Mr. Gould, De Barral) or egotistic vanity (Nostromo) isolates man no less than the romantic illusion of reality.

5. *The Rescue,* p. 142. Note the allusion to Don Quixote.

6. *Ibid.,* p. 215.

7. *Ibid.,* p. 339. D'Alcacer says:

> If we were murdered . . . he would fall under the suspicion for complicity with those wild and inhuman Moors. Who would regard the greatness of *his day-dreams, his engaged honor, his chivalrous feelings?* . . . it would *morally* kill him.

Ibid., p. 405-406. My italics.

8. *The Rescue,* p. 444 and p. 435. Also: "It was but a cruel change of a dream. Who could tell what was real in this world?" *Ibid.,* p. 431. "She [Mrs. Travers] gave him a *waking dream* of rest without end, in an infinity of happiness without sound and movement, *without thought,* without joy." *Ibid.* My italics. Mrs. Travers saw on Lingard's face, "which should have been impassive or exalted, the face of a stern leader or the face of a *pitiless dreamer—* an expression of utter *Forgetfulness.*" *Ibid.,* pp. 217-218. My italics.

9. *Ibid.*, pp. 116, 466.

10. *Ibid.*, p. 285. My italics. Also: "She saw herself standing alone, at the end of time, on the brink of days." *Ibid.*, p. 151.

11. *The Arrow of Gold*, p. 69. My italics.

12. *Ibid.*, p. 98. My italics.

13. *Ibid.*, p. 147.

14. *Ibid.*, p. 340.

15. *Ibid.*, p. 350. My italics.

16. *Chance*, p. 175.

17. *Ibid.*, p. 221. My italics. Also: "Solitude had been his [Anthony's] best friend. *Ibid.*, p. 364.

18. *Life and Letters.* I, 43-47. My italics.

19. *Chance*, p. 206. My italics. Also: "A young girl, you know, is something like a temple. You pass by and wonder what mysterious rites are going on in there, what prayers, what visions?" *Ibid.*, p. 311. Also: "Because men, I mean really masculine men, whose generations have evolved an ideal woman, are often timid—who wouldn't be before an ideal?" *Ibid.*, p. 268.

20. *Ibid.*, p. 324. My italics.

21. *Ibid.*, p. 348. My italics.

22. *Ibid.*, p. 331. My italics.

23. *Ibid.*, p. 326. My italics.

24. *Ibid.*, p. 329. My italics.

25. "A Smile of Fortune," "*Twixt Land and Sea*," p. 39. Also: "She was as much of a castaway as any one ever wrecked on a desert island." *Ibid.*, p. 59.

26. *Ibid.*, p. 64. Italics mine. Also: ". . . her tragic loneliness of a hopeless castaway." *Ibid.*, p. 82.

27. *Ibid.*, p. 65. My italics.

28. *Ibid.*, p. 79.

29. *Ibid.*, p. 86.

30. *Life and Letters*, I, 113.

31. *An Outcast of the Islands*, p. 334.

32. *The Rescue*, p. 322. My italics. Also: "Conflict of some sort was the very essence of his life. But this was something he had never known before. This was *a conflict with himself.*" *Ibid.*, p. 329. My italics. Lingard says to Mrs. Travers: "I only know . . . that wherever I go, I shall carry you with me—against my breast." *Ibid.*, p. 466.

33. *Lord Jim*, p. 11. My italics.

34. *Ibid.*, p. 340.

35. *Ibid.*, p. 176. My italics.

36. *Ibid.*, p. 93.

37. *Ibid.*, p. 323. My italics.

38. *Ibid.*, p. 343. My italics.

39. *Ibid.*, p. 339. My italics.

40. Thomas Moser, *Joseph Conrad: Achievement and Decline* (Cambridge, 1957).

41. Letter to S. L. Noble, *Life and Letters*, I, 184.

42. *Under Western Eyes*, p. 362.

43. Ludwik Krzyzanowski, "Joseph Conrad's Prince Roman."

44. Jan Lechon, "Adam Mickiewicz, A Critical Appreciation," *Adam Mickiewicz, Selected Poems*, edited by Clark Mills, (New York, 1956), p. 45.

45. Quoted by Maria Dabrowska in *Sketches about Conrad*, p. 20. My translation.

46. Juliusz Slowacki, *Dziela, Dramaty* (Works, The Dramas), (Wroclaw, 1952), p. 256. My translation.

47. *Ibid.*, p. 259. My translation. My italics.

48. *Nostromo*, "Author's Note," p. xiv. My italics.

49. *Ibid.*, p. xii.

50. *Ibid.*, p. xiii.

51. *A Personal Record*, p. 28. My italics.

52. *Lord Jim.*, p. 215.

53. *The Rescue*, p. 74. My italics.

54. *Lord Jim*, pp. 214-215. See also p. 334.

CHAPTER III

THE BALANCE OF COLOSSAL FORCES

1. "This is nature—the balance of colossal forces . . ." *Lord Jim*, p. 193.

2. *Typhoon*, p. 40. My italics. Also see *The Mirror of the Sea*, Initiation, p. 140, and p. 148.

3. Letter to Henry S. Canby, April 7th, 1924. *Life and Letters*, II, 342. My italics.

4. *The Nigger of the Narcissus*, "To My Readers in America," p. ix.

5. *Typhoon*, p. 40. Also: "His heart, *corrupted by the storm* that breeds a craving for peace, rebelled against the *tyranny of training and command.*" *Ibid.*, p. 52. My italics. Conrad well knew this tyranny of command from his own experience; "MacWhirr," he writes, "is not an acquaintance of a few hours, or a few weeks, or a few months. He is the product of twenty years of life—my own life." *Ibid.*, "Author's Note," p. viii.

6. "I understood the loneliness of the men in charge." *The Mirror of the Sea*, p. 70. Also: "A sense of catastrophic loneliness overcame my inexperienced soul." *Ibid.*, p. 126. In a book which is no less autobiographical than *The Mirror of the Sea*, we find

similar passages: "Ships have been dismasted. . . And I am shrinking from it. From the mere vision. My first command. Now I understand that strange sense of insecurity in my past. I always suspected that I might be no good. . ." *The Shadow Line*, pp. 106-107.

7. *Ibid.*, p. 106. My italics.
8. *Ibid.*, p. 93.
9. *Ibid.*, p. 62. My italics.
10. "Heart of Darkness," p. 116. My italics.
11. *Ibid.*, p. 144.
12. *Ibid.*, p. 82.

CHAPTER IV

THE ANATOMY OF BETRAYAL

1. *Notes on Life and Letters*, I, 26.
2. *An Outcast of the Islands*, p. 276. Also p. 275.
3. *Ibid.*, pp. 334-335. My italics.
4. "Amy Foster," *Typhoon*, p. 113.
5. *Ibid.*, p. 132.
6. *Ibid.*, p. 142.
7. *Under Western Eyes*, p. 301. "Betray. A great word. What is betrayed? They talk of a man betraying his country, his friends, his sweetheart. There must be *a moral bond* first. *All a man can betray is his conscience.*" *Ibid.*, p. 37. My italics. Lord Jim holds a similar trial of himself: "His answers seemed to shape themselves in anguish and pain within his breast—come to him poignant and silent like *the terrible questioning of one's conscience.*" *Lord Jim*, p. 28. My italics. Said Conrad himself: ". . . it would take too long to explain the intimate alliance of contradictions in human nature which makes love itself wear at times the desperate shape of betrayal." *A Personal Record*, p. 36.
8. *Nostromo*, p. 439. My italics.
9. *Victory*, pp. 315-316.
10. *Under Western Eyes*, p. 358. My italics.
11. *Ibid.*, p. 368.
12. *Nostromo*, pp. 419-420.
13. *The Nigger of the Narcissus*, "Preface," p. xii. My italics.
14. *Victory*, "Author's Note," pp. x-xi.
15. *A Personal Record*, "A Familiar Preface," p. xiii.
16. *Letters from Conrad*, edited by Edward Garnett (London, 1927).
17. *Under Western Eyes*, pp. 10-11.
18. *Victory*, p. 199.

19. *Ibid.*, p. 140.
20. *Ibid.*, p. 222. My italics.
21. *Ibid.*, p. 298. My italics.
22. *Ibid.*, p. 406.

CHAPTER V

THE PERFIDIOUS HAND OF FATE

1. "The Return," *Tales of Unrest*, p. 134.
2. *Victory*, pp. 353-354. My italics.
3. *Under Western Eyes*, "Author's Note," p. viii.
4. *A Personal Record*, "A Familiar Preface," pp. xvii-xxi.
5. "Falk," *Typhoon*, p. 236. My italics.
6. On December 6, 1894. Quoted by Jerry Allen, *The Thunder and the Sunshine*, p. 210. My italics.
7. *Life and Letters*, I, 269.
8. Alice Raphael, *Goethe the Challenger* (New York, 1932).
9. *Victory*, p. 379.
10. *Nostromo*, p. 301. My italics.
11. *Lord Jim*, p. 321. My italics.
12. *Victory*, p. 201.
13. Mr. J. H. Buckley gives several instances in Victorian literature, where fire is the visible means of purgation, e.g., Rochester in *Jane Eyre*, Krook's spontaneous combustion in *Bleak House*, etc. See J. H. Buckley, *The Victorian Temper*, "The Pattern of Conversion" (Cambridge, 1951).
14. "The Return," *Tales of Unrest*, p. 137.
15. *Ibid.*, p. 186. A *Flammentod* image once more.
16. *Nostromo*, p. 522. A *Flammentod* phrase again. My italics.
17. *Chance*, p. 312.
18. *Ibid.*, "Author's Note," p. xii. Also: "We are victims of the destiny which has brought us together." *The Rover*, p. 117 ". . . a ridiculous fatality." *Nostromo*, p. 155.

CHAPTER VI

THE EXPERTS IN THE PSYCHOLOGICAL
WILDERNESS

1. *The Shadow Line*, p. 62. My italics.
2. *Ibid.*, pp. 131-132.
3. *Chance*, p. 311.

4. *Lord Jim*, p. 50. My italics. Note how Marlow identifies himself with Jim's (and Conrad's) ideal of fidelity and moral standard of conduct.

5. *Ibid.*, pp. 50-51. My italics.

6. *Ibid.*, My italics.

7. *The Rescue*, p. 309. Also: "his [D'Alcacer's] secret aloofness from the life of men . . ." *Ibid.*, p. 283. Conrad compares D'Alcacer's detachment to that of Jörgenson.

8. *Lord Jim*, p. 213.

9. *The Rescue*, p. 408.

CHAPTER VII

PURELY HUMAN

1. Letter to Alfred A. Knopf, July 20, 1913. Quoted in Alfred A. Knopf's article, "Joseph Conrad: A Footnote to Publishing History," *The Atlantic Monthly*, Vol. 201, No. 2 (February, 1958), p. 64.

2. Walter Kaufmann, editor, *Existentialism from Dostoyevsky to Sartre* (New York, 1956), p. 11.

3. Jeal-Paul Sartre, *Nausea* (Norfolk, Connecticut, 1959), p. 165.

4. Letter to Cunninghame Graham, January 31, 1898, *Life and Letters*, I, 226.

5. *A Personal Record*, p. 92.

6. Jean-Paul Sartre, *Extentialism and Humanism* (London, 1948). This book is a lecture delivered in Paris in 1945; published in French in 1946 while Sartre was in the U. S. Subsequently it was disavowed by him as too one-sided in its apologetics.

7. *Ibid.*, p. 55.

8. *Letters from Conrad*, p. 265.

9. Jean-Paul Sartre, *Intimacy and Other Stories*, translated by Lloyd Alexander (New York, 1948), pp. 134-135.

10. *Ibid.*, p. 136.

11. Irving Howe, "Conrad: Order and Anarchy," *Politics and the Novel* (New York, 1957).

12. David Riesman, "Some Types of Character and Society," *The Lonely Crowd* (New Haven, 1950), p. 3.

13. Letter to George T. Keating, December 14, 1922. *The Portable Conrad*, p. 753.

14. *Ibid.*

INDEX